BRIGH'

TESS OF THE D'URBERVILLES BY THOMAS HARDY

Intelligent Education

INFLUENCE
PUBLISHERS

Nashville, Tennessee

BRIGHT NOTES: Tess of the d'Urbervilles

www.BrightNotes.com

No part of this publication may be used or reproduced in any manner whatsoever without written permission, except in the case of brief quotations in critical articles and reviews. For permissions, contact Influence Publishers http://www.influencepublishers.com.

ISBN: 978-1-645424-88-8 (Paperback)

ISBN: 978-1-645424-89-5 (eBook)

Published in accordance with the U.S. Copyright Office Orphan Works and Mass Digitization report of the register of copyrights, June 2015.

Originally published by Monarch Press.

Robert William Ackerman, 1964

2019 Edition published by Influence Publishers.

Interior design by Lapiz Digital Services. Cover Design by Thinkpen Designs.

Printed in the United States of America.

Library of Congress Cataloging-in-Publication Data forthcoming.

Names: Intelligent Education

Title: BRIGHT NOTES: Tess of the d'Urbervilles

Subject: STU004000 STUDY AIDS / Book Notes

CONTENTS

1) Introduction to Thomas Hardy   1

2) Textual Analysis
   Chapter 1–13   7
   Chapter 14–28   25
   Chapter 29–35   45
   Chapter 36–42   62
   Chapter 43–48   78
   Chapter 49–53   98
   Chapter 54–59   115

3) Character Analyses   131

4) Glossary of Dialect Words,
   Foreign Expressions and Difficult Words.   141

5) Summary of Criticism   148

6) Essay Questions and Answers   158

7) Bibliography and Guide to Research   166

INTRODUCTION

. . . .

LIFE OF HARDY

Thomas Hardy, the son of a building contractor, was born in 1840 in a small town in Dorset, in southwestern England. He attended church regularly with his family, and later taught in the local Sunday school. As a boy he memorized all the services, and this knowledge underlies the frequent references to religion in his works. In addition, Thomas' father was a musician who played at church services, and the boy followed in his father's footsteps by learning to play the violin. This was the start of a lifelong interest in music, which also figures prominently in his books. Although young Hardy's education was not particularly good, there were books in his home and he read all he could. At the age of sixteen, he left school and was apprenticed to an architect. Hardy is thus one of the relatively few well-known English writers who did not have a university education (Shakespeare and Dickens are others). Although his formal studies stopped, he continued to educate himself. He would arise early in the morning and study for an hour or two before leaving for work. In this way he continued to read various Latin and English authors and also taught himself Greek. In 1862 he left the architect's office, well trained as a draftsman and with a considerable amount of reading behind him. At the age of twenty-two he left Dorset for London. There young Hardy came into contact for the first time with the advances of the modern world. It must be understood that life in the Dorset of the 1840's and 1850's had hardly changed in its broad outlines since the Middle Ages. It was nearly completely rural in character, and at that time was still, sufficiently isolated from the rest of the world for few of the industrial and mechanical aspects of modem civilization to have come to it. (Dorset provides the setting for most of Hardy's novels and stories, including those that are generally thought to be his best. Hardy, however, changed the name of Dorset to "Wessex," and he changed the names of all the towns he wrote of as well. A map of the Wessex country, with both the real and fictional names of the places that occur in Hardy's work, is to be found in the edition of *Tess of the d'Urbervilles* edited by Carl J. Weber—see Bibliography.) In London he worked as an architect. He also studied French, visited art galleries and the great London exposition, and continued his course of reading. During these years he wrote the first of his poems to survive. It is clear that he greatly expanded his mental horizons, but he paid a price for his excessive exertions-—his health suffered and he was generally unhappy. In 1867 he returned to Dorset, but not as a full-time architect. He temporarily stopped writing poetry and made his first attempt at prose fiction. Hardy had reached a real crossroads in his life. By 1868 he had completed his first novel—*The Poor Man and the Lady*—which, though it was rejected, convinced him that he should continue his efforts at novel-writing. In the same year he did his last work as an architect, and it was during this time that he met the girl he was to marry. It was altogether a most crucial year for Hardy.

HIS NOVELS

All Hardy's novels were written during the next twenty-eight years. *The Poor Man and the Lady* was a slashing social satire, and when it was rejected Hardy switched to writing romances, stories with complicated plots and much sensational action. He began with *Desperate Remedies* in 1871, *Under the Greenwood Tree* (1872) and *A Pair of Blue Eyes* (1873). These books are highly autobiographical (as are the first novels of most writers), and they were reasonably well reviewed. *Under the Greenwood Tree* was the first of the novels to have a rural setting. Before. *A Pair of Blue Eyes* appeared as a book, it came out as a serial in a magazine, and this set a pattern—nearly all the rest of Hardy's novels were first published in this form. (This was a common practice for novelists in general in the nineteenth century.) In 1874 he published *Far from the Madding Crowd*, the earliest of the novels which are generally read today. This book received very favorable reviews, and Hardy followed it with *The Hand of Ethelberta* in 1876. The latter work is not a pastoral novel because Hardy decided that he did not want to be identified in the. public mind as a writer who could only write about "cows and sheep." Throughout his novel-writing career Hardy was very sensitive to the reading public, and he often acknowledged that he sought popularity. The next book Hardy composed is certainly among his best and most popular— *The Return of the Native* (1878). This was followed by several volumes which are not among his most successful efforts: *The Trumpet-Major* (1880), *A Loadicean* A1881), and *Two on a Tower* (1882). By this time Hardy was recognized to be one of England's leading novelists, and this reputation was greatly enhanced by the books that appeared in the next decade. This period of Hardy's career saw the production of those novels that have ensured him lasting fame. In 1886 there was *The Mayor of Casterbridge*, in 1887 *The Woodlanders;* 1891 saw *Tess of the d'Urbervilles*, and *Jude the Obscure*, the last novel he wrote, appeared in 1896. (*The Well-Beloved* came out in 1897, but it had been written in 1892.) Throughout these years Hardy was composing short stories as well as novels, and several volumes of these stories appeared, as follows: *Wessex Tales* (1888), *A Group of Noble Dames* (1891), and *Life's Little Ironies* (1894). (A last book of stories, *A Changed Man, The Waiting Supper, and Other Tales,* came out much later, in 1913.) After *Jude the Obscure* Hardy mainly wrote poetry. It should be remembered that he started out as a poet and had been composing poetry throughout the time he was writing novels. The last novels he published were all very controversial, and they caused Hardy to undergo some very severe criticism. This criticism, which sometimes amounted to personal abuse, combined with his continuing love for poetry and his newly won financial security, caused him to abandon the novel and return to poetry. *Wessex Poems*, which contained some of his earliest work, came out in 1898 and was received very well. In 1901 he published *Poems of the Past and Present*. The first part of his great epic poem *The Dynasts* appeared in 1903. It deals with the Napoleonic Wars and is one of the longest poems in English. The second and third parts came out in 1906 and 1908. The satirical title of *Time's Laughing-Stocks* (1909) indicates something of the bitter tone of this collection of ballad-like poems about sexual infidelity and unsuccessful marriage. It is thought that Hardy's own marriage was not especially happy, but its tensions were not to last much longer. In 1912 his wife Emma died. Hardy expressed his deep feeling for her in several of the poems that made up his next collection of verse: *Satires of Circumstance, Lyrics and Reveries* (1914). Hardy was then seventy-two, and the loss of his wife was a great shock. His life seemed to disintegrate, and he passed through two disastrous, disorganized years. In 1914, however, he married again, and his life once more regained its balance. In the same year the First World War broke out, but it did not check his inspiration. He continued to write, and in 1917 brought out *Moments of Vision and Miscellaneous Verses*. He followed this by *Late Lyrics and Earlier* (1922), the verse drama *The Queen of Cornwall* (1923), *Human Shows* (1925), and finally *Winter Words*, published posthumously in the year of his death, 1928.

HARDY'S TIME

The age in which Hardy wrote, sometimes called the late Victorian period (after Queen Victoria, who reigned from 1837 to 1901), was one of great change and many difficulties. In fact, in the Victorian period we can see the beginnings of many of the problems of our own time. English society was experiencing severe strains in its attempts to adjust to vast alterations in its structure, and *Tess of the d'Urbervilles* reflects its author's concern with several of the most pressing problems of his time. Hardy depicts the effects of the pressure of the new, urban, and industrial civilization on the old, rural, and agricultural life of Wessex. He exposes the hypocrisy of the rules that govern sexual behavior and the position of women in society. The third leading theme of the book is the question, especially acute in his day, of how to live in a time when religion no longer provided acceptable rules of conduct. Both Angel and Alec are typical young men of the age, sufficiently enlightened to reject the traditional standards, but unable to create new ones for themselves. Thus both are alone in relation to their society. *Tess* is one of the first novels to examine this theme (a major one ever since) of the effects of spiritual and moral isolation in modem society. Of course *Tess* is a novel and not a textbook on morals, and therefore these problems are not taken up in a systematic way; rather, they form the background of ideas and feelings against which the characters move and act.

THE NOVEL'S STRUCTURE

The structure of the novel has often been discussed. Thomas Hardy was an architect by training, and it is tempting to suppose that this background may have caused him to plan his novels as carefully as we know he did. Before he began to write, he worked out a detailed outline, including a table of important dates in the lives of his characters (for such a table on *Tess,* see the appendix of Weber's *Hardy of Wessex*). In the past Hardy's structural craftsmanship has often been praised, but today opinion has changed. Present-day critics still believe that a novel requires careful planning and construction, but they now think that the reader should not be aware of the craftsman at work. In Hardy, the reader is all too often conscious of the details of the structure (it is as if one were aware of all the carpentry in a house). Take, for instance, the rather mechanical alternation between spring and fall, and the fact that Tess is arrested at Stonehenge on June 1, just five years to the day that she set out to visit Trantridge. Nevertheless, if we do sometimes see the puppeteer a little too clearly behind the stage, there is no denying the cumulative power and effect of the tragedy that befalls Tess, and this is in large measure due to the careful plan of the book, obvious or not.

TESS OF THE D'URBERVILLES

TEXTUAL ANALYSIS

CHAPTER 1–13

. . . .

Tess of the D'Urbervilles is divided into seven parts, or "phases," as Hardy calls them, each of which is further divided into chapters, there being fifty-nine in all. The phases bear titles, but the chapters do not. *Phase the First*, which contains eleven chapters, is called "The Maiden."

PHASE ONE ("THE MAIDEN"): CHAPTER ONE

The book opens on a May evening. A middle-aged man walking to his home in the village of Marlott (in southwestern England) meets a local parson who addresses him as "Sir John." As the man is anything but a knight ("I be plain Jack Durbeyfield," he says), he is puzzled and asks for an explanation. The parson replies that he does historical research as a hobby, and in his investigations he has discovered that plain Jack Durbeyfield is in fact the last descendant of the d'Urbervilles, an ancient noble family with a long and distinguished past. Unfortunately the d'Urbervilles had come upon very bad days and had been forced to sell all their vast estates and property; indeed, Durbeyfield seems to be the last survivor of his branch of the family. Durbeyfield, a simple man who is a peddler and wagon driver by trade (called a "higgler" or "haggler"), is impressed by this information and begins to think of himself as "Sir John d'Urberville," The parson leaves, not at all sure that he has done the right thing in telling him. Durbeyfield decides to try to live up to his new identity and therefore sends for a carriage to take him the rest of the way into Marlott. In the village, the "women's club-walking" is going on.

Comment

The parson realizes that telling Durbeyfield might have a bad effect, but as he says when he decides to tell him: "Our impulses are too strong for our judgment sometimes." These words state one of the leading **themes** of the book: the conflict between passionate impulse and reasoned judgment. That this first link in the long chain of tragic events in Tess should be an ill-advised action is wholly in keeping with Hardy's idea (which he states throughout the book) that life is usually hostile, and at best neutral and indifferent, to man's purposes and desires; man can expect bad luck much more often than good.

PHASE ONE: CHAPTER TWO

The "club-walking" is the survival of an ancient custom that Hardy tells us was once common throughout England. In it the women of the town, all dressed in white, parade to the main square and there do a dance. One of the "walkers" is Durbeyfield's pretty, innocent, sixteen-year-old daughter Tess. She is "at this time of her life a mere vessel of emotion, untinctured by experience." She is embarrassed when her father comes riding through the village in his rented carriage singing of his new "title"; she thinks he is drunk (a not unusual state for him). Her friends tease her a bit, but when the dancing is about to start he is forgotten. At that moment, three young men of the upper class (they are brothers) happen to come through Marlott on a walking tour, and one of them, named Angel, decides to take part in the dancing. He chooses a partner, and as he begins to dance, he spies Tess, standing on the edge of the circle without a partner. He regrets not having chosen her, and she regrets not having been chosen. They exchange an eloquent look, but after only one dance Angel must leave in order to catch up with his brothers who have gone on ahead. As he goes, he turns back to take a last look at the pleasant village scene, and he sees Tess gazing after him.

Comment

The "club-walking" is like the more familiar practice of dancing around the Maypole, and like Maypole dancing dates back to pre-Christian times in England (before the sixth century), when the people worshiped fertility gods. The ceremony is a "gay survival from Old Style days-when cheerfulness and May-time were synonyms-days before the habit of taking long views had reduced emotions to a monotonous average," filled with a joy and directness of feeling that Hardy believes are no longer to be found in England. In general Hardy dislikes modern life, and throughout the book those characters and objects that represent it are depicted as debased and inhuman (for example, Alec d'Urberville or the steam-driven harvester). For all its beauty, however, the club-walking is basically insignificant because it has lost its connection with the ancient pagan life that gave it meaning, and it persists basically as a social custom.

The chapter is important because in it we meet two of the main characters in the book - Angel and Tess. It is significant that the first time they meet, Tess is wearing a white dress, which symbolizes her purity. Here Angel doesn't choose her because he doesn't see her until he has picked a partner. Later, when they marry, Tess again wears a white dress. This indicates that despite her experiences with Alec (see chapter eleven) she is still pure. (For Hardy, it is purity of spirit that is important.) Then, too, Angel does not really see Tess until it is too late, and for the second time their paths diverge.

When Angel overlooks Tess, Hardy ironically comments that the d'Urberville "pedigree" "did not help Tess in her life's battle as yet, even to the extent of attracting to her a dancing partner.... So much for Norman blood unaided by Victorian lucre." Notice that for Hardy life is a "battle." More important, Hardy is saying that there are different kinds of nobility: Tess is of the true nobility (that of "Norman blood" - Norman refers to the Norman conquest of England in 1066, in which the d'Urbervilles were supposed to have taken part); Alec Stoke-d'Urberville, whom she meets in chapter five, is of the false kind (that of "Victorian lucre"); and Jack Durbeyfield is somewhere in the middle, a representative of the true nobility much debased. A further **irony** of this passage lies in Hardy's remark that being a d'Urberville has not helped Tess "as yet"; of course, being a d'Urberville leads to her undoing, and never helps at all.

PHASE ONE: CHAPTER THREE

Tess leaves the dance and goes home to see what has become of her father. At home she finds her mother, Joan, washing clothes and taking care of her six younger brothers and sisters. The house appears drab and depressing to Tess, especially after she has been exposed, if only for a few moments, to Angel's refined manners. Her mother, who is a simple, vain, weak, and superstitious person, tells Tess that her father has just come from the doctor, who has told him that he has a bad heart condition. She also tells Tess what Mr. Durbeyfield has learned concerning the family's connection with the noble d'Urbervilles, and she informs Tess that her father is at Rolliver's tavern celebrating his ancestry. Since Mr. Durbeyfield has to make a delivery the next day that will require him to start well before dawn, Tess asks her mother to fetch him from the tavern. Mrs. Durbeyfield goes but does not return. Tess then sends her young brother Abraham to bring them both home, and when he has been gone for quite some time, she decides to go to Rolliver's herself.

Comment

Jack and Joan, Tess's parents, are the names traditionally associated in England with farmers (compare Jack and Jill of the nursery **rhyme**); by giving them these names Hardy indicates that the Durbeyfields are average rural working people and that his story has a validity and truth not limited by the specific circumstances of the action.

Tess, we learn, has graduated from high school ("completed the Sixth Standard in National School"), which was by no means common for a rural girl of the time. (This does not contradict Hardy's earlier statement Tess was "a mere vessel of emotion" because "emotion" there was not being contrasted to "reason" but to "experience.") Her mother, on the other hand, believes in fortune-telling books, and the letters she writes later in the novel are barely literate. It is this gap between them that Hardy

BRIGHT NOTES STUDY GUIDE

refers to when he says: "When they were together the Jacobean and the Victorian ages stood juxtaposed." The Jacobean age was the first quarter of the seventeenth century; the Victorian was the second half of the nineteenth century (when Hardy was writing) - the implication is that Tess is a modern girl. Tess seems to embody the best elements of both eras; her mother has only the old, traditional knowledge considerably weakened and largely inappropriate to the new, modern world.

PHASE ONE: CHAPTER FOUR

Mrs. Durbeyfield had found her husband at the tavern and together they had imagined a fine future for themselves and especially for Tess as a result of their new-found noble "connections." It seems that there is a wealthy Mrs. d'Urberville living near Trantridge (at no great distance from Marlott) who they suppose must be a member of a junior branch of the family. Mrs. Durbeyfield has settled upon the idea of sending Tess to her to "claim kin" (announce that they are related). Once this has been done, Mrs. Durbeyfield thinks, good fortune is bound to follow.

Tess finally gets her parents' home late at night, and to no one's surprise Mr. Durbeyfield is in no condition to make the long trip early the next morning. Mrs. Durbeyfield asks Tess and Abraham to go in his place. They start out long before dawn, and the old horse slowly picks his way along the road while Tess and her brother, neither fully awake, talk and daydream about the future. Suddenly they are jolted awake. The mail coach has crashed into their unlighted wagon, and their horse has been killed. Tess feels the accident to be her fault; had she been more attentive, it never would have happened. As she watches the horse die, she thinks of herself as a "murderess."

Comment

As young Abraham begins to wake up, he looks about him and sees "strange shapes assumed by the various dark objects against the sky; of this tree that looked like a raging tiger springing from a lair; of that which resembled a giant's head." These threatening images are (as often in this book) omens of the disaster that is soon to follow: in this case, the death of the horse. The entire incident is an omen of what will result from attempting to "claim kin." There are several similarities between the death of the horse and later events: Tess tries to help the dying animal and is splashed with blood as a result, just as at the end of the book she will be splashed with Alec's blood; both Alec and the horse die from wounds in the breast. By "killing" the horse Tess destroys the family's livelihood, its means of survival; by killing Alec she does the same thing again but she also loses her life. Hardy remarks that the hole in the horse's chest looked barely large enough to let his life pour out, and this is an ironic **foreshadowing** of the insignificance of Tess's tragedy in comparison with the huge scale on which nature works.

Hardy emphasizes the isolation of the two children (for Tess is barely more than a child at this point), when he speaks of the stars "coldly" shining "in serene disassociation from these two wisps of human life."

Significantly, Abraham asks Tess just before the accident whether the Earth is a "splendid" world or "a blighted one." Tess replies: "A blighted one."

After the horse dies, and Tess regards herself "in the light of a murderess," we see her beginning to change; she is no longer the innocent girl she was when she danced on the village green.

PHASE ONE: CHAPTER FIVE

The death of the horse finishes the family's hauling business. Tess, who had not been at all enthusiastic about her mother's plans for making contact with Mrs. d'Urberville, now feels guilty about the horse, and agrees to go and see their "cousin." Unknown to the Durbeyfields, however, the d'Urbervilles are not d'Urbervilles at all. Their real name is Stoke, and they are a family that made money in business and adopted d'Urberville only because it was the name of a noble but supposedly extinct family; indeed, they call themselves "Stoke-d'Urberville." Tess arrives at their imposing mansion and meets handsome, forceful, twenty-three-year-old Alec Stoke-d'Urberville. She embarrassedly explains why she has come. Alec is very attracted by Tess and seeks to sweep her off her feet by showering her with attention and with hothouse flowers and other delicacies. He also promises to see whether he can do something for her family. Tess is too innocent to understand why he is interested in her, and she leaves for home unaware of Alec's "wicked" intentions. The chapter ends with Alec's chuckling to himself at the strange turn of events that has given him such a pretty "cousin."

Comment

The Stoke-d'Urberville house is situated next to "one of the few remaining woodlands in England, of almost primeval date, wherein Druidical mistletoe was still found on aged oaks." (See Glossary.) It is ironic that this setting of great antiquity should surround the home of the newly rich and falsely noble Stoke-d'Urbervilles. As one would expect, the Stoke-d'Urbervilles have nothing to do with tradition. The grounds of the estate are "bright" and shiny, and, symbolically, the chicken coop Tess is later to work in was formerly a farmer's cottage. The fact that it had been a human habitation for hundreds of years has no importance to upstarts such as they are.

The Stoke-d'Urbervilles are representatives of the barbarians who in the past were conquered and ruled by the true aristocracy, the old d'Urbervilles. The main characteristic of modern life for Hardy is the complete breakdown of the old relationships which used to prevail between men. Alec, who is described as having "touches of barbarism" in his features, will subdue Tess, the true nobility. Alec's barbarism reflects his sensual nature and also serves to oppose him to Angel, Tess's other lover, in physical terms.

The ruin that Tess is soon to experience at the hands of Alec is heavily underscored and anticipated in this, her first meeting with him. A thorn on one of the roses Alec gives her scratches her skin, a bad omen. On another level, Hardy speaks of "the 'tragic mischief' of her drama" and of how she was "doomed to be seen and marked and coveted that day by the wrong man." Again, at the end of the chapter he speaks of how nature rarely manages to bring together the two people most suited to one another.

PHASE ONE: CHAPTER SIX

Having spent the night at the home of an acquaintance, Tess returns home the next day to find that "Mrs. d'Urberville" (whom she did not meet) has written to offer her a good position working on the estate's poultry farm. In addition, Alec has been at the Durbeyfield house, and has charmed everyone. Mrs. Durbeyfield's imagination has been sparked by the appearance of Alec, and she is now certain that he will fall in love with Tess and "make a lady of her." The entire family now puts pressure on Tess to accept the job, but she is hesitant because somehow she doesn't "quite like Mr. d'Urberville." Her sense of obligation to her family wins out, however, and she suppresses her suspicions of Alec and accepts the offer.

Comment

At every turning point in the story there is something that keeps Tess heading in the fatal direction. Here it is the pressure of her family combined with the guilt she feels about the horse.

PHASE ONE: CHAPTER SEVEN

The next morning Tess prepares to depart. After packing she comes downstairs dressed in everyday clothes. Her mother, however, is not satisfied with her appearance and insists on dressing her in her Sunday best, fussing over her until she looks especially beautiful. The entire Durbeyfield household (except Tess) is now positive that Alec will marry her. Tess sadly bids her father farewell and is instructed by him to tell Alec that he will sell him his "title" for one thousand pounds. He then lowers the figure to one hundred pounds, then to fifty, and finally to twenty pounds. Tess, miserable at her father's foolishness and lack of pride, leaves the house quickly. Her mother and sisters accompany her to the point where a cart from the d'Urbervilles is to pick her up. As she is about to enter it, a gig (a small carriage) darts out of the bushes and stops beside her. It is driven by Alec, who tells her to get in. Somewhat against her better judgment, she obeys and in a moment is out of sight. That night, in bed, Joan Durbeyfield has misgivings for the first time. She wonders whether it would not have been better to find out what kind of man Alec was before sending Tess. However, she manages to console herself by telling her husband that Alec is sure to marry her.

Comment

Mrs. Durbeyfield cannot understand Tess's hesitations because she regards marriage to a person of the upper classes as so desirable that personal dislike and moral considerations are nonexistent. She feels that sexual attraction is the best (perhaps the only) way to get a husband, which is, in her mind, the main thing every girl is interested in. Her moral principles are expressed in these words she says to Jack: "If he don't marry her afore he will after."

PHASE ONE: CHAPTER EIGHT

Alec and Tess travel along, with Alec paying her a constant stream of compliments. Soon they reach the top of a long steep hill and Tess, who has been nervous about traveling on wheels since her accident with the horse, asks Alec to go slowly. He makes fun of her fears and tells her his horse is wild and loves to race along. They start down the hill at full speed, and Tess is forced to put her arms around Alec's waist in order to stay aboard, but she removes them as they reach the bottom. This action annoys Alec, and when they come to the next hill he speeds up to force her to embrace him again. She refuses. He tells her he will slow down if she permits him to kiss her. Tess is greatly distressed but, desperate to make him stop, agrees. However, when he leans over to collect his kiss, she involuntarily moves aside. Alec is furious and speeds up again. Tess begs him to stop, promising that she will not move this time. He kisses her and she instinctively wipes her cheek with her handkerchief. This infuriates Alec and he again starts racing downhill. He says he will not stop until she permits him to kiss her again and promises this time not to wipe it off. Tess agrees, but just as Alec is about to kiss her, her hat blows off. She jumps off the gig, and after fetching her hat refuses to get back in. She tells Alec she will walk the rest of the way. Alec realizes that she has purposely allowed her hat to blow off and expresses his anger in foul language. Tess is shocked at his words and tells him she hates him. When he sees her angry his temper subsides, and he tells her that if she will only remount, he will never again drive fast against her will. Tess no longer trusts him, and she refuses to get back in. Thus, Alec must content himself with driving alongside Tess as she walks along the road to their destination.

Comment

When Tess wipes her cheek after Alec's kiss, he tells her that she is "mighty sensitive for a farm girl!" The point is that Tess is of the true, "instinctive" nobility, and Alec is "mighty insensitive," because he is made of coarser stuff than she is.

During the ride Tess is Alec's captive, **foreshadowing** the events of chapter eleven, when again he has her at his mercy, and then is able to have his way with her. Hardy always describes Alec in sensory terms and images in contrast to the intellectual and artistic portrait of Angel later in the book.

PHASE ONE: CHAPTER NINE

Upon her arrival at the Stokes, Tess is shown the birds she will be caring for. One of the servants tells her that "Mrs. d'Urberville wants the fowls as usual." Tess does not understand what this means, but simply follows the maid, who also tells her that Mrs. d'Urberville is blind. Each of them takes two birds to Alec's mother, who is in the sitting room of the main house. She greets Tess cordially and immediately takes one of the fowls from her. She touches it and then identifies it, calling it by name and feeling it all over to see if it is all right. After having satisfied herself with regard to all the birds, she than asks Tess whether she can whistle. Tess says yes, but not well, so Mrs. d'Urberville asks her to practice because she wants her to whistle to her finches. It seems that when the finches hear tunes they learn to sing them, but lately they have heard no new tunes. The maid reminds her that Alec had whistled to them that morning, but upon hearing her son's name a frown crosses Mrs. d'Urberville's face. (Although she loves him, she knows him for what he really is.) Later that day, Tess tries to practice whistling. Suddenly Alec appears and proceeds to teach her how to whistle. She is grateful to him. As time passes Tess comes to feel more relaxed with Alec, although she never comes to like him much more than she did at first.

PHASE ONE: CHAPTER TEN

The main pleasure of the working-class people of the area is to go on Saturday nights to a nearby market town, and there drink and generally have a good time. After Tess has been at the d'Urbervilles for a while, she agrees to go on one of these outings with some of the villagers. Finding that she enjoys herself, she goes with them often after that, but even when she goes to town alone she always waits to return with everyone in order to avoid having to make the long walk home alone. One Saturday night, she waits and waits, but no villagers appear. She goes to look for them and finds them drunk and dancing wildly. Alec

BRIGHT NOTES STUDY GUIDE

d'Urberville appears and offers to take her home, but Tess, still uncomfortable with him, refuses. He tells he to suit herself, and finally the villagers, many of them drunk, begin walking home. On the way, one of the village girls, Car Darch (nick-named "the Queen of Spades" and one of Alec's old girl friends), gets into an argument with Tess, accusing her of thinking herself better than the rest of them because Alec is favoring her "just now." She wants to fight with Tess but Tess indignantly refuses; when the other women threaten her, she forgets her fears and determines to walk home alone. She has gone but a few feet when Alec rides up and asks what the fight is about. When no explanation is forth-coming he tells Tess to jump up behind him on his horse and he will take her home. Tess, desperate to get away, and against her better judgment, agrees. As they speed away into the night, Car Darch's mother laughs and says, "Out of the frying pan into the fire."

Comment

The sensuality of the dance anticipates the sensuality that is shortly to come (between Alec and Tess). The dancers cavort with wild abandon; they are compared to Pan and Syrinx and again to Priapus and Lotis: both these references to Greek mythology involve the sexual pursuit (and capture) of a chaste young maiden by a sensual male god.

PHASE ONE: CHAPTER ELEVEN

As they ride along Alec asks Tess why she minds his kissing her. She answers that she supposes it is because she doesn't love him. She says she is often offended when he tries to make love to her. They ride along but Tess doesn't realize that they have missed the turning for Trantridge. Weary, she dozes for a moment and leans against Alec. He puts his arm about her waist and she, alarmed, pushes him. He is angered and tells her he was only trying to keep her from falling. She apologizes, and he asks if he may treat her as a lover. He then puts his arm around her waist and doesn't permit her to protest. Suddenly Tess realizes that they have long since passed their turning. She berates Alec for his treachery in misleading her and begs to be let down so that she may walk home. He agrees, but only on the condition that she let him go and find where they are, for he too is lost. She accepts his offer and dismounts. He makes a bed for her in some leaves. He mentions, casually, that he has given her father a new horse and has sent some toys to her brothers and sisters. Happy for her family but disturbed by her feeling of indebtedness to Alec, she lies down on the leaves, and he goes off. Having recognized a landmark, he returns to find Tess asleep. He lays his cheek against hers and finds tears on her eyelashes. And in the night and the silence the Tess who left her mother's side is first changed and then gone forever. (Hardy means that they have sexual intercourse; he could not be more direct because of the attitudes of the time in which he was writing.)

Comment

It is noticeable how most of the emotional and passionate scenes in this book take place at night or in twilight, and the climactic action of this first phase is no exception. Significant, too, is the fact that it takes place in the primeval woods; that is, in a place which goes back to a time before manmade ideas of morality ever existed and which thus has nothing to do with such ideas. It also takes place in the fog, when it is difficult to see, and important differences are blurred. (Compare the recurrence of the fog in Part Four, Chapter 31.) This pattern is in accord with Hardy's idea, expressed throughout this book, that Nature is unconcerned with man's desires and works only to satisfy its own purposes, which it does through our emotions and not through the reason. It is to be understood that Tess has not been raped or forced: it is the night, the atmosphere, her fatigue, Alec's attractiveness (which she feels although she doesn't like it), and her ignorance of sex (she says later that she didn't know what he was doing until it was too late) that causes the seduction to occur.

PHASE TWO ("MAIDEN NO MORE"): CHAPTER TWELVE

One Sunday morning in October, shortly after her "experience" with Alec, Tess packs her bags and leaves the d'Urberville household. After walking for miles she reaches a hill from which she can see the valley in which her home is situated. At this moment Alec drives up and expresses annoyance at her leaving without telling anyone. He offers to drive her the rest of the way and she agrees. When they come into sight of Marlott she begins to cry. She says that she despises herself for her weakness, particularly because she does not love Alec at all. Alec says he is willing to provide for her but she refuses indignantly. After accusing her of being overly high and mighty, he admits that he is bad and will probably die bad; he promises, however, that never again will he be bad to her. He tells her he will help her should she be in need. Tess gets out of his gig, resignedly receives a last kiss from Alec, and begins to walk the last part of the way to Marlott. On the way she meets a man with a pot of red paint on his arm, who tells her he does most of his work on Sundays. This activity is explained when, leaving her for a moment, he walks over to a fence and paints in large letters the words "Thy Damnation Slumbereth Not." The sight of the words causes Tess to be overwhelmed with guilt, and she asks the man whether he believes what he has written. He states emphatically that he does (he also says that he began his painting because he was inspired by a Reverend Clare, who will be an important character later). Tess is appalled by the texts he is painting and tells herself that she cannot believe God ever said such things as the man is writing. In a moment she is home, and her mother expresses great surprise at seeing her. Weeping, she tells Joan all that has happened. Her mother characteristically chides her for not having gotten Alec to promise to marry her and accuses Tess of selfishly disregarding the welfare of the rest of her family. Tess replies that she was unaware that men could be dangerous and asks her mother why she hadn't prepared her more adequately to meet the realities of life. Mrs. Durbeyfield, at last aware of the part she has played in her daughter's difficulties, simply counsels her to make the best of it.

Comment

For simple Mrs. Durbeyfield, "Nater" (nature) is "what do please God." This easy connection of the demands of nature and the demands of morality could only be made by someone as unthinking as Tess's mother. Hardy is also asking: What kind of God is it that can be pleased by men and the things they do to one another?

PHASE TWO: CHAPTER THIRTEEN

Tess is the center of curiosity in Marlott, and for a short time she is borne along on her friends' interest. Then she is seized by a deep depression. She is tortured by visions of her ruined life. She goes to church once and feels herself the subject of gossip. This state is unbearable to her, and henceforth she remains indoors during the day. Only at twilight does she go out, and then she takes long walks at night. She feels herself to be closely entwined with nature, so that she interprets a rainy day as "an expression of irremediable grief at her weakness" in the mind of God. Hardy says that her misery was wholly unnecessary because it was created by her own mind - "a cloud of moral hobgoblins by which she was terrified without reason." For, Hardy says, while she felt herself to be the personification of Guilt, she was in reality no such thing. "She had been made to break an accepted social law, but no law known to the environment in which she fancied herself such an anomaly."

Comment

As was noted above, passionate acts (and therefore in the eyes of conventional morality, guilty acts) and committed in the dark, while the daylight is the time when the conventional morality has control. Thus Tess, in her wretchedness, can only feel free and unrestrained once twilight comes: "She had no fear of the shadows."

Hardy's comments on the relations between man, nature, and society emphasize certain **themes** already announced; the clash between impulse and reason in man (impulse is "natural," reason is "learned") and the characterization of Tess as "a mere vessel of emotion."

TESS OF THE D'URBERVILLES

CHAPTER 14–28

. . . .

PHASE TWO: CHAPTER FOURTEEN

It is the following August, harvest time. Tess is now a field laborer, but, more important, she is a mother. Her feelings about her baby are mixed: she both loves and hates it. After the birth of the baby, Tess has shaken off her misery and begun to come back into the world, and thus she has taken work as a harvester. When she returns home from work, she finds the baby is ill, and it soon becomes apparent that it will die. Tess is frantic because it has not been baptized. She wants to go to the parson but her father, drunk, forbids her. She is desperate. Then she gets an idea-she will baptize the baby herself: "Perhaps baby can be saved! Perhaps it will be just the same!" She awakens her brothers and sisters, who kneel as she performs the ceremony by flickering candlelight. She christens the child "Sorrow." The child dies. Tess then plucks up her courage and asks the parson whether the baptism is valid. He is undecided, and finally says it is. She then asks whether Sorrow can be buried in the church

BRIGHT NOTES STUDY GUIDE

cemetery. He permits this as well, and so Tess's child is laid to rest.

Comment

The action throughout the book is associated with the seasons of the year. Tess goes to the d'Urbervilles in the spring, and her "ruin" at the hands of Alec takes place in the summer. As the year declines, so does she. She returns home in October, and the barren winter is the time of her misery. Gradually she revives as the world of nature does. This pattern can be observed elsewhere.

In the description of the harvesters, Hardy says that "a field-woman is a portion of the field; she has somehow lost her own margin, imbibed the essence of her surrounding, and assimilated herself to it." That is, women, because of and through their emotional nature, tend to give themselves more unreservedly to their surroundings than men do. Hardy often makes such general statements about women. Observe in this connection how Tess seems to become part of Angel later.

Hardy again says that the root of Tess's situation lies in the conflict between human morality and physical nature: her child is said to be "that bastard gift of shameless Nature who respects not the civil law." Note that the impressive, emotional baptism scene takes place at night.

PHASE TWO: CHAPTER FIFTEEN

Tess remains at home during the winter following the death of her child. She holds herself aloof at Marlott, and thus interest in her dies down. Nevertheless she realizes she can never be comfortable there again. Next May when she hears of a job as a dairymaid at a farm "many miles to the southward," she accepts it.

Comment

Tess has matured as a result of the pressure of the events of her life: "Almost at a leap Tess thus changed from simple girl to complex woman." Note again how Tess responds to natural rhythms and urges: she breaks out of her dull and sterile existence when "a particularly fine spring came around, and the stir of germination was almost audible in the buds; it moved her, as it moved the wild animals, and made her passionate to go." None of the men in the book has this direct and natural response to Nature.

PHASE THREE ("THE RALLY"): CHAPTER SIXTEEN

Tess sets out on foot for Talbothays dairy, in which she will be working. It is a glorious May morning, and Tess is delighted by the beauty of the landscape through which she is walking. After a walk of some miles she finally comes to the Valley of the Great Dairies, which is "intrinsically different" from her native valley, Blackmoor Vale.

Comment

The differences between Blackmoor Vale and the Valley of the Great Dairies reflect the differences between Tess's lovers in each. Both are beautiful, but Blackmoor is "heavy … luxuriant"; the new valley is "clear, bracing, ethereal." These correspond to Alec and Angel, respectively.

PHASE THREE: CHAPTER SEVENTEEN

Tess meets Mr. Crick, master dairyman of Talbothays, and is immediately put to work milking. At the barn she meets Angel Clare, whom she recognizes as the man who did not choose her as his partner at the club-walking; but he does not recognize her. He is Mr. Crick's pupil, learning dairying in preparation for a life as a farmer. He is the son of Reverend Clare, a poor parson at the other end of the county, and is described as "educated, reserved, subtle, sad, differing."

Comment

The name "Angel" is ironically appropriate. Angel is good, and he is ethereal (spiritlike) as we might expect an angel to be; as a man, however, he leaves much to be desired, as we shall see.

PHASE THREE: CHAPTER EIGHTEEN

In this chapter we learn Angel's background,. He is the youngest son of Reverend James Clare, one of the last of the strict devout, old-fashioned clergymen. His father intended him, like his brothers, for the university and a career as minister, but Angel's was independent in thought-so independent, in fact, that he became an atheist. When his father discovered this, he refused to send him to the university, and Angel decided to become a farmer. He has been studying the various aspects of agriculture and has come to Talbothays for six months to learn dairying. When he had first arrived at the dairy, he had kept himself aloof, but gradually he began to mix with the others. Somewhat to his surprise he found that he enjoyed their company and the outdoor life that they led. He began to change, to grow away from his old ways of thinking; and he especially began to become sensitive to the rhythms of nature. For the first few days after Tess's arrival, Angel does not notice her because she is so quiet. Gradually, however, as she becomes accustomed to the life at Talbothays, she begins to "open up." He is first attracted by the "fluty" quality of her voice (he is an ardent musician). Once she has gained his attention, he observes her closely and soon realizes that she has extraordinary qualities for a milkmaid. Dimly he thinks he must have met her before, somewhere in his travels about the countryside.

Comment

There are many similarities between Angel and Tess. Both love music; both are religious but not in the conventional sense; both have had sexual "adventures" in the past which were uncharacteristic of their lives in general (Angel had two days of dissipation in London some years before during a crisis caused by his religious doubt). In this chapter Angel makes the first move toward "choosing" Tess, after having overlooked her in chapter Two.

PHASE THREE: CHAPTER NINETEEN

To prevent his cows from becoming partial to one milker and thereby creating difficulties should that milker have to leave, Mr. Crick discouraged his helpers from favoring the cows that each found easiest to milk. Nevertheless, Tess finds herself getting the same cows every day. She soon discovers that this is Angel's doing. She speaks to him of it, and he remarks that it does not matter because she "will always be there to milk them." Tess warmly replies that she hopes she shall, thinking, of course, of her secret and of the seclusion she has found on the farm. Later she regrets her words and the emotion with which she said them. She fears that Angel now thinks that her desire to stay is somehow related to him. Suddenly she hears the sound of a stringed instrument coming from the nearby garden. She realizes that Angel is playing, and in the warmth and beauty of the summer night his music appeals to her deeply. She steals close to where he is sitting and, hidden by the darkness, listens until tears come to her eyes. He stops playing and Tess waits, hoping he will start again. Angel, however, has been walking about as he plays, and when she moves he spots her light-colored gown. She draws back and he asks what she is afraid of. Of "life in general" is her reply. He tells her that that is his feeling also, and expresses surprise that a young girl should see things as he does. She tells him she envies him for being able to make music and thus rid himself of his fears. Angel is surprised that Tess, though only a milkmaid, shows such sensitivity. Tess, on the other hand, is surprised that Angel who seems to her to have everything necessary to happiness, should sometimes feel as she does, that life is not worth living. She cannot understand why a young man of such obviously intellectual lean should want to be a farmer. Thus, neither of them really has the information necessary to understand the other. Gradually they come to know more of each other, and Tess realizes the great intellectual gulf between them. She feels very dejected and he, discovering the reason for it, offers to teach her anything she wants to know. She tells him that what she'd really like to know is "why the sun do shine on the just and unjust alike." Once again Angel is surprised at the depth and tendency of her feelings. Nevertheless, she still feels greatly inferior to him in intellectual matters, and wishing very much to get his good opinion, she thinks of telling him her ancestry. Before she does this, however, she sounds out Mr. Crick on Angel's opinions about the nobility. Mr. Crick says that Angel is very unconventional in his thinking and indeed has very little use for old families at all. She is glad that she has not spoken, and she deduces that his interest in her derives from what he supposes to be "newness" in her.

Comment

In this chapter the relationship between Tess and Angel deepens and becomes much more intimate. The setting is very significant. It is a garden which is lush and luxuriant (like the rest of Talbothays), but this part of the garden is composed of weeds, weeds that stain and beslime everything. (Note, too, that there are apple trees in this garden.) In short, it is not too much to say that this garden resembles the Garden of Eden (see Chapter Three of the Book of Genesis in the Bible), particularly when we realize that in this scene a beautiful woman is accosted by an angel. (Hardy even gives Angel a harp.) Of course, Angel is hardly what his name implies; for as we shall see, he ravishes Tess even more (because he does it spiritually) than her first seducer Alec. The moment has a kind of magic to it. "Tess was conscious of neither time nor space." And, as we have come to expect, the scene takes place at night.

PHASE THREE: CHAPTER TWENTY

As the lush summer "develops and matures," so does the feeling between Angel and Tess. They are balanced on the verge of love for each other, studying each other, being drawn to each other, "converging, under an irresistible law, as surely as two streams in one vale." They meet continually in their work on the farm. Tess is given the task of awakening the rest of the milkers, and so at three o'clock every morning she awakens him. He dresses quickly and they are alone outdoors. To Angel, Tess seems to be more than human in her beauty, and he compares her to various Greek goddesses. As it grows lighter, Tess becomes again simply a beautiful woman, but Angel finds that her image remains in his mind.

Comment

The peculiar kind of "luminous gloom" in which Tess and Angel walk to the dairy shed each morning makes Angel's mind turn to the hour of the Resurrection; Hardy comments that "he little thought that the Magdalene might be at his side." At these moments, Tess looks "ghostly, as if she were a soul at large," "She was no longer the milkmaid, but a visionary essence of woman - a whole sex condensed into one typical form." In sentences and references like these, the plot as such is not really advanced, but in them we get a sense of Tess's stature, of her moral and spiritual magnitude.

PHASE THREE: CHAPTER TWENTY-ONE

"There was a great stir in the milk-house just after breakfast" because the milk would not turn into butter no matter how hard it was churned. Immediately the farm people begin to speak of similar situations having occurred in the past and how they handled them-in those days, they would go to the local "conjuror," or magician, to have the "spell" taken off the churn. Mr. Crick tells a story about how his churn was damaged some years ago. It seemed that one of the milkers, named Jack Dollop, who was a great ladies man and had made one of the milkmaids pregnant, had gone back on his promise to marry her. One day the maid and her mother came storming into the dairy to find Dollop. Terrified, he hid in the churn. The mother looked and looked and finally, somehow, found that he was in the churn and began to turn it. Dollop was flung about inside and badly bruised. She continued to do this until be agreed to marry her daughter. The story, naturally, disturbs Tess because of its resemblance to the events in her own life. She says she is feeling ill, and Mr. Crick begins to make a fuss over her; then the butter begins to come, and her reaction is forgotten.

Because June days start so early for the milkmaids, they usually go to sleep very early in the evening. This evening, Tess is first into bed and dozes until she is awakened by the talking of the three other maids who share the room. The three of them, Retty, Izz, and Marian, are standing at the window staring intently at something. From their words it soon becomes clear that the center of their attention is Angel, and that all three are desperately in love with him. They all agree that they would marry him tomorrow, but they admit that they haven't a chance "because he likes Tess Durbeyfield best." The little group at the window disperses as Angel goes indoors, and soon they are asleep. Tess is not. She has been stung by their talk: it was "another of the bitter pills she had been obliged to swallow that day." She knows that Angel is inclined toward her, and she toward him, but her heart is tortured because she feels that she could never conscientiously allow "any man to marry her now." Therefore she feels that she is doing wrong in diverting Angel's attention from other women during the brief period he will be at Talbothays.

Comment

Resorting to conjurors seems natural in Talbothays, which seems to be a throwback to a Golden Age of sheer vegetable energy. It seems to be a place where the worship of the old fertility gods would not seem out of place.

PHASE THREE: CHAPTER TWENTY-TWO

The next morning Mr. Crick says that the dairy has received a complaint from one of its customers - the butter has a strange taste. The dairyman tastes it and gives his verdict - garlic. Then some of the older hands remember that a few of the cows had grazed in a field that had once contained some garlic. Mr. Crick immediately sets everyone to weeding the field of all traces of the offending herb. Angel, who makes it a rule to participate in everything, finds himself, not by accident, weeding alongside of Tess. Distressed by what she has heard the night before, she makes a noble effort to praise Izz and Retty to Angel, commending their persons and their skills. However, Angel isn't interested in hearing praise of anyone but Tess. From this day forward, Tess forces herself to take pains to avoid him, never allowing herself to remain alone in his company for any length of time. She resolves to give the others every chance she can. Tess comes to realize from what she knows of the other dairymaids' feelings that Angel has the honor of all of them in his keeping, and her respect for him increases as she observes that he never does anything that might compromise any of them.

PHASE THREE: CHAPTER TWENTY-THREE

It is now July, and the valley in which Talbothays is situated swelters with heat. It is Sunday, and for the past twenty-four hours the valley has been drenched by driving rains. Had it been any day but Sunday, the maids would have had no problem with the footing, but on Sunday of course they dress up to go to church. And that means that they wear thin shoes instead of their everyday wooden shoes. Therefore when the girls come to a place on the road to church which has been washed out by the rains, they are in a quandary as to how to get through. At this moment they spy Angel coming toward them, and their hearts beat faster. Angel, of course, is not a churchgoer, and in fact he has been out early that morning seeing what effect the rain has had on the hay when he spies the girls and approaches them. As soon as he sees the huge patch of mud and water that is blocking their path, he suggests a solution-he will carry them across. He immediately puts his plan into effect, carrying first Marian, then Izz, and then Retty through the water. When he lifts Tess, he tells her he has undertaken the first three-quarters of the labor so as to enjoy the last quarter-holding Tess in his arms. He strides out into the water with her, and then his emotion gets the best of him. He exclaims, "O Tessy!" Tess's heart leaps, and she cannot answer because of the pressure of her feelings. He feels he ought not to take further advantage of the accidental position, and thus no more definite profession of love is made by either of them. It is, however, perfectly clear to the other three girls what the truth is. Yet, because of their affection for Tess and because "they had been reared in the lonely country nooks where fatalism is a strong sentiment," they yield to Tess and are not malicious toward her.

Tess now cannot deny the reality of her love for Angel. The fact that he is loved by the others only makes him more precious to her. She tells her friends, however, that she will refuse him if he asks her to marry him, as she would refuse any man. But she says she thinks the issue will never come up because she doesn't think he is interested in marrying now at all. These words of Tess's smooth things over, and the four girls are friends once again. That night, the bedroom of the girls "seemed to palpitate with their hopeless passion." They all are in the grip of an impulse-sexual attraction-which has been imposed on them "by cruel Nature's law." "The differences which distinguished them as individuals were abstracted by this passion, and each was but a portion of one organism called sex." Each recognize the futility of her love from a social point of view. Hardy says that such love lacks "everything to justify its existence in the eye of civilization" but lacks "nothing in the eye of Nature." The four toss and turn on their beds, and after a while, recognizing that they are not going to be doing any sleeping, they begin to talk. Tess now hears for the first time that Angel's family has picked out a girl for him to marry, a girl of his own rank and background. Once she hears this she entertains no further "foolish thought" that Angel is serious in his attentions to her. In her mind it now seems clear that the whole matter is a passing summer infatuation.

Comment

Again and again throughout this novel Hardy takes great pains to oppose Nature's purposes to those of man and to contrast the tiny scale on which man acts with the vast one of Nature. Thus, here, the girls are submerged in the tide of sexual attraction and fertility which is universal and is at work everywhere (the animals, the crops at the dairy). It is against this vast and indifferent background of nature that the tragedy of Tess is played out.

PHASE THREE: CHAPTER TWENTY-FOUR

July wore on, and the state of the weather seemed to be Nature's attempt to "match the state of hearts at Talbothays." As Angel is oppressed by the outward heat, so is he burdened by the rising tide of his passion for "the soft and silent Tess." Everyone and everything at Talbothays is governed by the overpowering heat. Activity slows to a minimum; even the cows are milked in the fields, without even being driven back to the dairy shed. On one of these scorching afternoons several of the cows move away from the rest of the herd at milking time. Among them are several of the animals that Tess always milks. She follows them behind the hedge where they have gone and beings to milk one of them. She is not aware that Angel has come up behind her and is watching. The sun is shining on her face in the quiet of the afternoon, and all that can be heard is the milk squirting into the pail in response to the action of Tess's "pink hands," which move "as if they were obeying a reflex stimulus, like a beating heart." Her face is wonderfully appealing to him; she seems to be the embodiment of life. Angel trembles with the intensity of his feeling, and sneezes. Tess thus becomes conscious that he is there, observing her. The quiver that led to the sneeze intensifies until finally all reticence and reserve are overcome. He comes to her and takes her in his arms. Taken by surprise Tess reacts naturally and sinks into his embrace with "something very like an ecstatic cry." He asks Tess to forgive him for "taking liberties." Her eyes fill with tears. He asks her why she is weeping, and she replies that she doesn't know. Angel says, "Well, I have betrayed my feeling, Tess, at last ... I love you dearly and truly." Angel unconsciously understands "that his heart had outrun his judgment." They both go back to milking, but for better or worse the situation between them is unalterably changed.

Comment

Hardy says, after Angel's declaration of love, that had Mr. Crick known what had taken place he would have "despised" it "as a practical man." Nevertheless, Hardy states that the passion that had shown itself in the pasture was "a more stubborn and resistless tendency than a whole heap of so-called practicalities."

Nature works in us through that part of our selves which we share with all the rest of the animal creation; it is for this reason that Angel's "heart had outrun his judgment."

PHASE FOUR ("THE CONSEQUENCE"): CHAPTER TWENTY-FIVE

That night Angel sits and thinks about the events of the day. He can hardly grasp the change that has come about between him and Tess, much less be clear about how they should act when others were about. He reflects on the extent to which his ideas about life have changed. Hitherto he has shared the common notion that nothing very important happens to people of the lower social classes, that in fact such people were barely distinguishable one from another. Now life has proved him wrong. He realizes that "life was to be seen of the same magnitude here as elsewhere."

Angel, despite his faults, is "a man with a conscience" (as opposed to Alec), and he realizes that he cannot trifle with Tess and her feelings, That is to say, he cannot continue to meet her in the ordinary way because their continued contact will cause their love to grow. This he cannot permit unless he is prepared to take the consequences: i.e., marry her. Since he has come to no firm conclusion on this matter, he decides that until he does, he should avoid her presence. He therefore determines that he will leave Talbothays for a short while and go to see his family.

As he rides along the road that leads to his home in Emminster, Angel asks himself whether he ought to marry Tess- whether he dares to marry her. He is very uncertain about the reaction of his family, and indeed about his own reaction some years hence if he does marry her. Will he regret it? Is this simply a matter of physical attraction that is bound to decline once the magical moment has passed? He enters Emminster with these thoughts in his mind; as he does so, he sees at the end of the street Miss Mercy Chant, the girl whom his parents hope he will marry. She is devout and learned in theology, a Sunday School teacher in the town. She passes by without seeing him, and he enters the Clare house. He has not advised anyone that he is coming, and therefore everyone is excited as well as delighted to see him. Here we meet Angel's parents, and especially his father. Reverend James Clare is a clergyman of the old school, of a type that is no longer common. Theologically he is an extreme adherent of the doctrines of John Calvin, the sixteenth-century Protestant theologian: that is, a rigorous and rigid system that asserts that some persons are chosen by God for salvation, and all the others have no possibility of being saved. "He had in his raw youth made up his mind once for all on the deeper questions of existence, and admitted no further reasoning on them thenceforward." More important than his theology perhaps is the complete sincerity and uprightness that pervade every aspect of his life. Within his limitations, Reverend Clare is that rare creature, a good man. He has no idea how distant his way of thinking and feeling is from that of Angel, particularly after Angel has been living in lush, pagan, sensuous Talbothays.

Living at the dairy has changed Angel, and his family is immediately aware of it. He has become more free and easy, more natural. He walks with his brothers, both of whom are clergymen, and they seem to him impossibly conventional and constrained. Neither has any life in him, and neither has any idea of how life is really lived by the vast majority of his countrymen who are neither clergymen nor university men. After their rather unsatisfactory talk, the three brothers return home for dinner. Angel has brought some blackpuddings and mead as gifts from Mrs. Crick, and naturally enough he expects them to be served. Mrs. Clare says, however, that the puddings were given to some parishioners who were ill, and the mead was found to be so alcoholic that it was deemed fit only for the medicine chest. Angel regrets the mead because, as he says, "that mead was a drop of pretty tipple." The rural expression mystifies the rest of the family, and summarizes the changes that have come over Angel during his time at the dairy.

Comment

As with other characters the name of Miss Mercy Chant tells us something about her and permits us to "place" her. She is obviously religious and is as lifeless and wan as Angel's brothers; like them, she is perfectly proper. Her undoubted virtues count for nothing in Angel's mind when they are set alongside those of the "impassioned, summer-saturated heathens in the Var Vale." Throughout Tess, Hardy deprecates religion. It is either a lifeless affair, as with the Clare family; or a matter of fanaticism, as with the text painter or those who are followers of Alec later in the book. Its main quality for Hardy is that it shuts men off from reality, which is to be found in the natural world around us. The pale, thin, life-denying quality of the Clare family is brought out well in the incident of the puddings and mead.

PHASE FOUR: CHAPTER TWENTY-SIX

After evening prayers Angel finds an opportunity to discuss with his father several matters close to his heart. He first speaks of his plans to enter farming, and his father then tells him that he has felt it his duty to set aside some money each year for the purchase of a farm because he has not had to pay for Angel's university education. This topic leads Angel to one related to it: marriage. His father agrees that Angel, being twenty-six, has reached the time to think of taking a wife. Angel asks what kind of wife his father thinks would be best for him as "a thrifty hard-working farmer." His father replies that she should be "a truly Christian woman," like Mercy Chant for example. Angel asks, however, whether he ought not be practical and marry a woman who will be able to help him with the work of running the farm. James Clare, who has never thought of this, dubiously agrees, but continues to argue that the main consideration is that of the girl's faith and religion. Finally Angel says that he has found a girl who seems to have every quality necessary for a farm wife. She is skilled in farmwork, serious of mind, and is a "church-goer of simple faith"; added to all this, she is surprisingly beautiful. His mother, who has entered during this conversation, asks whether Angel's bride is "a lady." Angel says that though she may be of undistinguished ancestry (he does not yet know of her being a d'Urberville), "she is a lady, nevertheless-in feeling and nature." Angel's parents, seeing how determined their son is, decide to go along with him and ask only that he not act in a hurry and that he bring her home so that they may meet her. The matter is dropped for the time being. Angel realizes that while his parents will see Tess from a middle-class point of view and will be concerned about her family, he sees Tess's "vital features." "It was for herself that he loved Tess; her soul, her heart, her substance-not for her skill in the dairy, her aptness as his scholar, and certainly not for her simple formal faith-professions." His experience at Talbothays has made him see that a person's worth is not a matter of class or family or anything of the kind; it is, rather, dependent on the inner aspects of the person, which arise without regard to material considerations.

Angel leaves Emminster, and his father rides with him part of the way back to Talbothays. The father passes the time by telling his son about how old-fashioned he is thought to be by his fellow-clergymen in his insistence on getting to a sinner directly and causing him to reform from within. Old-fashioned or not, says James Clare, his approach works. He tells Angel of many conversions he has made - but there have been failures too. One of these was a "young upstart squire named d'Urberville." It seems that, a knowledge of Alec's wicked life having reached the ears of the clergyman, he took it upon himself to speak out boldly from the pulpit on d'Urberville's behavior. D'Urberville resented this attack and proceeded to insult him publicly in a bitter fashion. For all his insults, d'Urberville is still a subject of Reverend James Clare's prayers, and the good clergyman still expresses hopes for his conversion. Angel thinks that his father has always been optimistic and idealistic. Although he cannot agree with his father's religious position, he admires him as a man. Despite his own lack of faith Angel feels himself closer to his father "on the human side" than are his two brothers, who being clergymen themselves should presumably resemble their father.

Comment

After having established Tess's "new" life in Talbothays, Hardy now brings back Alec to our attention. And, as so often is the case, the incident in which we see Alec foreshadows what is to come. Alec has attacked the father as he will shortly, in a much more serious way, attack the son.

PHASE FOUR: CHAPTER TWENTY-SEVEN

After a ride of some hours Angel finds himself descending into the valley in which Talbothays lies. He rejoices in the intimate knowledge he has of life on the dairy; returning to the farm after a visit to his parents' home "affected him like throwing off splints and bandages." It is the heat of the afternoon and not a person is to be seen. He enters the farmhouse and encounters Tess. She has just awakened and doesn't know he is there. She yawns and stretches; to Angel she appears as the essence of "femaleness." "It was a moment when ... the most spiritual beauty bespeaks itself flesh." Then she becomes conscious of his presence. He tells her he has hastened back to be with her, and they embrace. They go to the milkshed to do the skimming of the cream, and there Angel asks her to marry him. Griefstricken, she replies: "I cannot be your wife." Angel is astounded and presses her to explain her refusal. She will not and only repeats that she loves him but cannot think of marriage. Angel says that she must have more time to think about it, and the subject is dropped for the time. Tess is very distressed by what has occurred. Angel tells her of the events of his visit home, and especially of his father and his high principles. He tells her of the incident involving Alec d'Urberville and his father, but does not mention Alec's name. Tess, however, recognizes Alec from the story, and the memory of the past sweeps over her. Hopelessly she says: "It can't be!" She leaves the shed and joins the other dairymaids in the pasture where the cows are feeding. Now that Tess was again present in the flesh before him, it seems natural for Angel "to choose a mate from unconstrained Nature, and not from the abodes of Art."

Comment

The two ways of life symbolized by Emminster and Talbothays stand in sharp contrast to one another. The one is religious and sterile, the other pagan and lushly fertile. The home of Angel's parents is on the cool heights, while the dairy is down in the hot valley. At Emminster everyone lives a measured, controlled life; at Talbothays the farm girls move "with the bold grace of wild animals."

PHASE FOUR: CHAPTER TWENTY-EIGHT

After a few days Angel asks Tess why she refuses him so definitely. She says she "is not good enough." He says that she need not worry if she is fearful that his parents will not like her because she is only a farm girl. She cannot explain further, and Angel is genuinely puzzled by her behavior. She repeats that she loves him with all her heart, but she is "sure" that she ought not to marry him. He cannot understand, and he thinks it must be her shyness and unsureness at entering a higher social class. He assures her that all will be fine, particularly as she has in fact learned much from him, and has copied his vocabulary and even his accent. Meanwhile Tess is torn in her heart because she so much wants to say yes, but she forces herself to stick to the decision made by her conscience. Her friends, even Mr. and Mrs. Crick, have sensed what is taking place between her and Angel, and the two are often left to themselves. One day, when they are engaged at breaking up the curds in the milk, Angel again asks her to marry him or at least to explain why she will not. Tess is desperate because she feels her will power leaving her, and to gain time she promises to give him her reasons the next Sunday. She is tortured by the mixture of desire and denial that she is experiencing; she feels herself slipping slowly over to acceptance of Angel's love and of marriage. Despite her efforts to resist, she is gradually being carried closer and closer to the fulfillment of her deepest wishes. The days pass, and finally it is Saturday, the day before that Sunday on which she must declare herself. That night she knows she will say yes, although she knows she is doing wrong: "I can't bear to let anybody have him but me! Yet it is a wrong to him, and may kill him when he knows!"

. . . .

PHASE FOUR: CHAPTER TWENTY-NINE

The next morning at breakfast dairyman Crick says he has heard of Jack Dollop again; it seems that he has married a widow. Angel asks how it came about that Dollop did not marry the girl he had promised to wed after his bruising experience in the churn (see Chapter Twenty-one). Apparently, he has been paid in his own coin; he married the widow because she had an income of fifty pounds a year, but after they were married she told him that her income ceased when she married. The maids offer their opinions as to the rightness of what the widow did. When Tess is asked, she says that the widow should have told Dollop the truth or else refused to marry him. Someone else tells a joke and her words are forgotten, but she is miserable because of the obvious similarity between the story of Dollop and the circumstances in her own life. Angel comes up to her after breakfast and again asks her to marry him. He puts his arm around her waist in preparation for kissing her when she says (as he expects) yes. But Tess, still disturbed about the tale of Dollop and the widow, says no. He is surprised and releases her waist. "It all turned on that release" because her refusal, caused by the story, would "have been overcome in another moment. But Angel said no more; his face was perplexed; he went away."

Several weeks pass. Angel has changed his tactics. He no longer continues to ask her outright to marry him, but rather tries to coax her into accepting him. He is always there, by her side, always arguing his case. Tess knows she must break down because her love for him is growing until it is boundless. The end of summer is approaching, and early one morning Angel asks her firmly for an answer. "Is it to be yes at last?" She evades him again. They go out, following the other men and maids. Tess tries for one last time to divert Angel's attention from herself by praising the other girls, but the time is long past for that now. Angel shrugs off her noble attempt at sacrifice, and Tess is glad. Somehow she knows that it will be decided today. That afternoon milking progresses slowly, so slowly that it soon becomes apparent that the dairy will not be able to get the milk to the evening train unless someone drives there quickly. Angel volunteers to go, and Tess goes with him.

Comment

Another omen of things to come is seen in the story of Dollop and the widow. It exactly forecasts, in a comical way, the disaster that lies in store for Tess because she will insist on telling that which, in the world's eyes, ought not to be told.

PHASE FOUR: CHAPTER THIRTY

Angel and Tess are so absorbed in being truly alone with each other that they are not prepared for the rain that begins to fall in the twilight. Tess has not taken any outer clothing, and she becomes cold as the rain continues. Angel tells her to move closer to him, and he wraps them both in a large piece of canvas. He reminds her of his question, which she has promised to settle that day. She agrees that she will speak before they return to the farm, and they drive on in silence. To pass the time he begins to speak about a house they happen to be passing: "... an interesting old place ... which belonged to an ancient Norman family formerly of great influence in this country, the d'Urbervilles." Tess makes no comment. They finally arrive at the small railroad station, where there were "intermittent moments of contact between their secluded world and modern life. Modern life stretched out its steam feeler to this point three or four times a day, touched the native existences, and quickly withdrew its feeler again, as if what it touched had been uncongenial." They deliver the milk and then start back into the rain, huddled together under the canvas. Immediately Angel begins on the subject of marriage. She tells him that she has something to tell him-about her life before she came here. She says that once he knows it he will not like her so well. She briefly sketches her youth at Marlott and then says there was something else. "I - I was -" She does not know how to continue. All the while Angel, who is completely oblivious of what she might say, is encouraging her, helping her along in a somewhat patronizing way. At the last moment, Tess loses her nerve and says: "I - I - am not a Durbeyfield, but a d'Urberville." "And is that all the trouble, dear Tess?" "Yes," she answers faintly. She tells him Mr. Crick had told her that he hated old families, and thus she was afraid to tell him because it might make him love her less. He says the news does nothing of the kind; in fact, it is extremely interesting (because he can use it to impress his parents). "And this was the carking secret!" He laughs about what he now regards as having been a tempest in a teapot, and then casually makes the connection between the name of d'Urberville and the man who had insulted his father. Tess is very disturbed at this and says that she doesn't want to be known as a d'Urberville. Angel then gallantly offers her his name as an escape from d'Urberville. "If it is sure to make you happy to have me as your wife, and you feel that you do wish to marry me, very, very much -" She finally agrees to marry him, and as soon as she does so she bursts into sobs. Angel gently teases her for sobbing at what should be a joyous moment. Then Tess falls to kissing him passionately. They drive on toward the farm. Tess says she wishes to write to her mother, and Angel finally connects the name Marlott with the place he had passed through years before on the walking trip. He realizes that he has seen her before, and Tess says, "I hope that it is of no ill-omen for us now!"

Comment

Several things we have seen before come together in this important chapter. Angel and Tess express their emotions directly and intensely, and as we have come to expect in such a scene, the events take place in the evening and night. The opposition between the artificial life of the modern city civilization and the natural life of the rural life is expressed in the lines already quoted about the railroad and its weak hold on the countryside. Then, too, the omens that have been coming thick and fast in recent chapters continue here when, at the moment Angel is asking Tess to be his wife, Alec d'Urberville's name comes up, followed by the remembrance of the scene early in the book in which Alec passed up Tess for another partner. Finally, there is a curious echo here in Tess's ride with Angel of the ride earlier (in Chapter Eleven) with Alec. Both times she rides at night, pressed right up against the man to whom she yields herself.

PHASE FOUR: CHAPTER THIRTY-ONE

Tess writes a "most touching and urgent" letter to her mother in which she sets forth the situation she finds herself in. In a few days an answer from Mrs. Durbeyfield arrives. She tells Tess not to be a fool and therefore not to tell Angel-what he doesn't know won't hurt him. She says that similar situations arise continually, even among women in the highest born families, and since they don't trumpet their troubles, there is no reason for Tess to do so. The letter makes Tess realize how differently she and her mother see life, but she decides that her mother's advice is probably best. Having decided on a policy of silence, partly as a result of her mother's counsel, Tess grows calmer. The months of autumn are a time of near ecstasy for Tess, who now devotes herself wholly to her love for Angel. For her he is barely human and certainly faultless, so highly does she esteem him. She had never known a man who was at all like Angel, so kind, so intelligent, so protective, so spiritual; and he grows in her eyes every day. They are together all the time now, for constant companionship is the custom during rural engagements. Angel can hardly wait to inform his family of the ancestry of his bride-to-be. They talk for hours about their plans for the future, and Angel tells her that they will certainly leave this part of England, and that they may well leave England altogether. She can barely reply, so lost is she in her love for Angel. Her love for him acts to blot out the memories of the past in her, but she is always aware that her forgetfulness is only temporary, that the doubts, fears, and shame were only "waiting like wolves just outside the … light." One night, when the two of them were sitting indoors, she suddenly exclaims that she is not worthy of him. Angel won't hear of it, and Tess has to fight down her real feelings. She exclaims that she wishes he had selected her at the village dance years ago in Marlott. He doesn't understand why, and she, "with the woman's instinct to hide," says that in that way she would have had four more years of his company, four more years of happiness. Angel gently reproaches her with being flighty, and she says she is not-by nature. He says he wants to ask her a question. She tells him to ask and she will try to answer. "When shall the day be?" He suggests they be wed in two weeks, but the closeness of the date frightens her. She asks for a later date, but the discussion goes no further because Mr. and Mrs. Crick come into the room. Tess is embarrassed to be found so close to Angel, but he calmly announces to the Cricks that they are to be married soon.

That night, when Tess comes up to her room to go to sleep, the other three maids are waiting up for her. They are not angry at all, merely unbelieving. They cannot really comprehend that it is all really to take place, that Tess is going to marry a gentleman. They come close to her and touch her, as if this will help them to understand the wonderful news. Tess is glad that they do not dislike her; she murmurs that he ought to be marrying one of the other girls because any of them is much better than she is. The others are incredulous. They all admit that Tess is their superior in every way. Tess suddenly has a fit of weeping, and they all comfort her. They all get into bed, and Marian says: "You will think of us when you be his wife, Tess, and of how we told 'ee that we loved him, and how we tried not to hate you, and did not hate you, and could not hate you, because you were his choice, and we never hoped to be chose by him." These words burn into Tess's heart, and she resolves to tell her past to Angel, despite her mother's advice. She is willing to have the world regard her as a fool rather than deceive the one person she loves more than life itself.

Comment

Angel is described as being "rather bright than hot-less Byrnnic than Shelleyan." Hardy means by this that Angel had not much of the physical and rather more of the spiritual in his make-up. Moreover, Hardy here indicates several characteristics which will operate to determine Angel's behavior later. He says that Angel "could love desperately, but with a love more especially inclined to the imaginative and ethereal; it was a fastidious emotion which could jealously guard the loved one against his very self." These traits of Angel must be kept in mind in order to understand Angel's reaction of repulsion to Tess's disclosure of her past.

Tess's helplessness in the face of her impending doom is indicated in the **imagery** used by Hardy in this chapter. Tess's past, and the feelings that it inspires in her, is compared to a wolf circling around a campfire just outside the light. Then again she is said to be a "girl of simple life, not yet one-and-twenty, who had been caught during the days of immaturity like a bird in a springe [trap]." The comparison of Tess to a helpless creature like a bird will be repeated again in chapter forty-one.

In addition, from what we have noticed already, the fact that it is now October should alert us to a downward turn in Tess's fortunes. Her life seems to follow the course of the year, improving with the spring, declining with the autumn. Compare the events that take place in October and the following months in Phase Two with those of the spring and summer in Phase Three.

PHASE FOUR: CHAPTER THIRTY-TWO

Tess wishes that she might continue in the state she is now in-
engaged to be married but never having to make the decision
to wed. Angel, however, is insistent upon setting a date, and he
continues to put the question to her. It is getting toward winter,
and the cows are calving, which means that there is less work for
the milkmaids. Angel tells her that Mr. Crick has assumed that
Tess will go with Angel when he leaves the dairy in the winter,
and Tess feels pressed to decide soon. Finally Tess decides and
fixes the date, December 31. Now that all is determined she feels
swept along by events and by Angel. She writes to her mother to
tell her the news and to receive whatever advice she can, but her
mother does not reply. In fact the decision to wed seems to be
filled with rashness and haste. Once Tess proposes to postpone
the wedding until after Angel has established himself upon
what is to be their farm. But Angel is unwilling to leave her for
any extended period because he is afraid that all the changes
that have come about in her as a result of his influence will
disappear. He wishes her to continue to gain in poise and social
assurance before presenting her to his parents, and he feels that
she would acquire these qualities if they were to live together
for some months until they should be permanently established.
He now decides that he wishes to learn the operation of a flour-
mill, and the proprietor of the old mill at Wellbridge has offered
him a chance to inspect its operation. He rides over to see what
it is like and returns to the dairy determined to spend some days
at the mill. What has decided him is that he has learned that the
mill was once part of the estate of one of the branches of the
d'Urberville family. He and Tess decide to go there immediately
after their wedding and remain there for two weeks.

One Sunday morning in December Izz asks Tess why the
banns were not announced in church that day, for they must

be called three successive Sundays and now there are only two Sundays left before the end of the month. But Angel explains to Tess that he plans to be married by license. (One could be married by calling the banns three consecutive Sundays in church or by license, which was more private and more expensive.) Tess is relieved that the banns will not be announced because she has been afraid that someone who knows her past will object to the marriage. Nevertheless, she feels uneasy because of this piece of good luck. Somehow she takes it as a possible omen of misfortune: "All this good fortune may be scourged out of me afterwards by a lot of ill. That's how Heaven mostly does." Everything, however, goes well. One day Angel sets her mind at rest about her wedding dress when he hands her some packages which contain an entire wardrobe of clothing. She is very touched by Angel's considerateness, and she goes upstairs to try on her new white gown. As she looks at herself in the mirror she suddenly remembers two lines from an old song that her mother used as a lullaby: "That never would become that wife/ That had once done amiss."

Comment

Just as the old year ends of December 31 and the new begins, so Tess's old life will be ending and something new take its place. But the words of the lullaby are ominous.

PHASE FOUR: CHAPTER THIRTY-THREE

Angel wishes to spend a day alone with her before they are married, and so he suggests that they make a few purchases in the nearest town together. It is Christmas Eve, and the town is covered with holly and mistletoe. That evening they return to the inn at which they have stopped, and Tess waits for Angel in the entryway as he goes to have the gig brought around to the door. Two men pass her and one stares at her. The other remarks Tess's beauty, and the one who has stopped to stare proceeds to recite the history of the affair between Alec and Tess. Angel comes in as the man is speaking and is infuriated at his words. He punches the man on the jaw, and it looks like a fight is about to start. But the man reconsiders, thinks better of it, and apologizes. Tess is very shaken by the scene, and as they drive home she asks, without knowing exactly why, that the wedding by put off. But Angel calms her down, and they each go to their rooms. Tess stays awake, and she hears, after some time, a noise coming from Angel's room, a sound of struggling. Tess rushes to Angel's room and knocks on the door. Angel reassures her, saying it was only a dream. In it he was fighting again with the man at the inn, and the noise she heard was Angel's fists beating on the pillow. He says he "is occasionally liable to these freaks in my sleep." This dream is the last straw for Tess. She resolves that she must tell Angel everything, and she sits down and writes a complete account of her past, addresses it to Angel, and slips it under his door. She has an uneasy night but when she comes down in the morning Angel greets her with his usual kiss. He says nothing about the letter, and she does not mention it either. She cannot understand whether he has silently forgiven her, and that her fears were foolish, or whether, in fact, he has ever read the letter at all. She looks into his room, but the letter is nowhere to be seen. The days pass, and it is now New Year's Eve, the wedding day. The farmhouse is decorated for the occasion, but the ceremony itself will be a quiet affair. No one has been invited from Marlott, and none of Angel's family has come either. Angel feels the coolness on the part of his family stems from his marrying a dairymaid, and he knows that he can overcome it when he reveals to them that Tess is a d'Urberville. As for Tess, the fact that Angel has made absolutely no reference to her letter has now convinced her that he has never seen it. Therefore she goes up to his room, looks around, and finds it. She had shoved it under the door, and it had gone under the carpet as well. He had never seen it. She feels that she cannot give it to him now, the day of the wedding and with all the preparations made. She destroys the letter. She is in a state of inner turmoil but, because of the stir and bustle the wedding, can barely find a minute alone with him. Finally she does, tells him that she wants to tell him of her faults. Angel, however, won't hear of it; he says they can exchange confidences once they are settled in their new lodgings. Then the two of them are taken up again by the whirl of preparations and can say no more. They make the trip to the church, and the ceremony is muted, there being only a dozen guests. During the trip back Tess is silent and thoughtful. She tells Angel that she feels that she has seen the old carriage they are riding in before, but she cannot remember where. Angel tells her it must be the legend of the d'Urberville Coach working upon her. Tess says she has never heard it, and inquires about it. Angel hesitates but finally tells her that a d'Urberville of the sixteenth or seventeenth century committed a terrible crime in the family coach. Since that time, he says, members of the family see or hear the old coach whenever... He breaks off, and asks Tess to change the subject as it is inappropriate to a wedding day. She asks whether d'Urbervilles see the coach when they are going to die or when they have committed a crime. Angel silences her with a kiss.

By the time they arrive back at the farm Tess is sad. She is tortured by guilt: does she have any right to be Mrs. Angel Clare? She prays to God, but it really is to her husband that she prays. She is engulfed by the violence of her love for him. The time comes for their departure for Wellbridge Mill. All the farm folk are standing at the gate, watching the pair leave. She sees Retty, Izz, and Marian looking sorrowful, and so she asks Angel to give each of them a farewell kiss. He does so, and she sees that its effects are unfortunate in that the feelings that the girls have been trying to subdue are now emerging. After the goodbyes have been said, and just before the wedded couple depart, the cock crows. The farm people are dismayed. As Angel and Tess drive off, Mrs. Crick says to her husband: "It only means a change in the weather, not what you think; 'tis impossible."

Comment

The omens of bad luck have been coming thick and fast as the climax approaches. First, there is the fight between Angel and the man who knows Tess's past. We feel that this means that Tess's past will catch up to her. Then too, Angel's bad dream and the fact that he often has troubled sleep during which he seems to act out whatever is disturbing him is a forecast of the sleepwalking in Chapter Thirty-seven. Next there is the legend of the d'Urberville Coach. Angel leaves the story unfinished so that we do not know on what occasions the members of the family see the coach, but Tess suggests it is when they commit a crime or when they are about to die. For Tess the crime in question is her experience with Alec plus the fact that she has not told Angel of them, but this is not the last crime in the book. In fact the legend prepares us for crime and death later on. The third omen is the cock crowing in midafternoon, which is certainly an unusual, even an unnatural, action, and which is felt by everyone to be a warning of evil.

PHASE FOUR: CHAPTER THIRTY-FOUR

Angel and Tess arrive at Wellbridge. Upon entering they find that the farmer who lives there has taken advantage of their presence to pay a holiday call elsewhere, and so except for a servant they are alone in the place. The old farmhouse depresses Tess, however. She is frightened by two lifesize portraits of women that hang on the staircase. The women portrayed look like witches; their features show arrogance, treachery, and ferocity. They are ladies of the old manor-d'Urbervilles. Added to their ugliness is the fact that Tess's fine features are detectable; in exaggerated form, in their faces. Tess is even more thoughtful and quiet than she has been up to now. Angel is rather playful, as befits a new bridegroom, but he also thinks that she is now his responsibility: "What I become, she must become. What I cannot be, she cannot be. And shall I ever neglect her or hurt her, or even forget to consider her? God forbid such a crime!" They sit at tea, waiting for their luggage to be brought from the dairy. It begins to rain, and Angel says that the cock knew the weather was going to change. Finally, at seven o'clock, a knock comes at the door. Angel goes, expecting the luggage, but returns with a small package. It is from his father and addressed to Tess. Inside is a case which contains a diamond necklace and some other jewels which had been left by a friend of the Clare family for the woman whom Angel would marry. Tess puts on the jewels, and Angel is overcome once again by her beauty. After another long wait, the messenger with the baggage, Jonathan Kail, arrives. Jonathan seems very depressed and he soon tells them that there have been sad events at the farm. Retty Priddle has tried to drown herself, and has been rescued just in time, and Marian has been found dead drunk in a field. These incidents tip the scale for Tess. That such innocent girls should suffer on her account is too much for her: she determines to tell Angel everything. They sit by the fire, and then Angel asks her whether she remembers that he said they would exchange confidences once they were married. It seems that he has something to tell her, something he had been thinking of telling her for a long time but was afraid to do for fear it might cause her to love him less. He tells her of the time when, beset by religious doubts and despair, he had gone to London and spent two days in "dissipation with a stranger." After it was over, he realized the error of his ways, and knew he would never do anything like it again. He feels, however, that Tess ought to know of it, and he is glad he has confessed. He asks her: Do you forgive me?" "She pressed his hand tightly for an answer." Now, of course, Tess feels that her confession has been made easier, and says that she in turn has something to tell as well. Angel cannot believe it is serious, but she assures him that it is. Then, their hands still joined, their faces practically touching, they sit before the fire, and she entered on her story of her acquaintance with Alec d'Urberville and its results, murmuring the words without financing, and with her eyelids drooping down."

Comment

This chapter marks the **climax** of the novel. It is the point toward which the entire action has been building. At the beginning of the chapter there are more omens of things to come. The portraits of Tess's ancestors, so witch-like in appearance, nevertheless resemble her. Then Jonathan's message that their marriage has caused Retty to try to drown herself and Marian to get drunk again warns of disaster. Finally, and most important, Angel makes his confession. The fact that he, too, has engaged in sexual "immorality" will make his rejection of Tess in the next chapter much more painful than it would ordinarily have been because Angel, for all his unconventionality, still shows himself to demand one standard of conduct for women and another for men, and because the similarity of their experiences has led her to believe that he will understand. The details Hardy gives to describe the scene during her confession are important. Angel and Tess are sitting before the fire, and the "glow" from the coals give "a Last Day luridness" to everything. That is, Hardy is saying that the scene resembles the Day of Judgment, which the Bible says will come at the end of days, at which time the good and the evil are judged for all time. And of course it is the day of judgment in Tess, too, for in the events of their wedding night Angel and Tess reveal themselves and are judged (by each other, Hardy, and the reader). The basic difference between Tess and Angel is indicated in this critical moment by the way Tess forgives Angel instinctively, wordlessly, as compared with the intellectual, unfeeling way Angel will not forgive Tess in the next chapter.

PHASE FIVE ("THE WOMAN PAYS"): CHAPTER THIRTY-FIVE

Tess concludes her story, and as she does the physical environment seems to respond. "The fire in the grate looked impish-demoniacally funny, as if it did not care in the least about her strait.... All material objects around announced their irresponsibility.... And yet nothing had changed since the moments when he had been kissing her.... But the essence of things had changed." Angel is stunned. He cannot believe what he has heard. Tess begs for him for forgiveness, reminding him that she has forgiven him for similar action. He agrees that she has, but he finds it irrelevant. He says the woman he has been loving is not Tess but "another woman in her shape." As Tess begins to realize what Angel's reaction means, she is griefstricken. She asks him whether they can live together, and he answers that he does not as yet know. She tells him that she is ready to do anything he thinks is right: "I will obey you like your wretched slave, even if [your order] is to lie down and die." Angel is so disturbed that he feels he must leave the room. He goes out and leaves Tess, stunned and crushed. She dimly realizes that he has left and she goes after him. After following him for some time, she catches up with him and asks him to tell her what she has done. He tells her he has sworn to himself not to reproach her, and she continues to plead for mercy. He tells her that he forgives her, "but forgiveness is not all." She asks him if he loves her, and he does not reply. He chides her with being the "belated seedling of an effete [worn-out] aristocracy," and associates her low social position with the fact that she has displayed "a want of [moral] firmness." She makes no answer to these remarks, and they walk on in silence. She says that she is willing to commit suicide in order to spare him trouble, but he tells her not to be silly and to go back to the mill and go to bed. When she comes in, she goes to their bedroom. Completely dulled by the chain of calamitous events that have occurred, she gets into bed and is soon asleep. Angel comes in much later and goes to her room to see if she is asleep. He is relieved to find her there. He suddenly feels tenderness for Tess, and he has a moment of indecision at the door to the bedroom. Turning to the door, he catches sight of one of the horrible d'Urberville women of long ago, and again sees the resemblance between her and Tess. This sight is enough to make him turn away, and he goes downstairs. He has a "sterile" expression on his face, the look of a man who is no longer in the sway of a great passion but who as yet has come to no new feeling to replace the old one. He thinks over again what has taken place that night, and again he cannot understand how Tess's virginal appearance could survive the defiled state of her heart. He goes to sleep as the "night ... unconcerned and indifferent" comes in: "the night which had already swallowed up his happiness, and was now digesting it listlessly; and was ready to swallow up the happiness of a thousand other people with as little disturbance or change of mien [expression]."

Comment

Now the dreadful **irony** in Angel's name begins to become clear. He is no divine being at all, as Tess had thought, but a man, and a poor specimen at that. He cannot forgive Tess as she has forgiven him. He shows himself, at this crucial time, to be little different from his family, whom he thought would look down on Tess because they judge by appearances while he looks deeper, into the heart. He cannot recognize that she could not have become to him what she is unless her love reflected her deepest self. He cannot understand that Tess does not share his own separation between body and spirit but that she is a whole person. It must be remembered too that Angel's actions have a more than personal significance. He is, we have been told, a typical-example of a modern young thinking person, one who does not accept the traditional attitudes toward life but rather tries to understand life and live it in his own way. And, in fact, he is such a person-he has changed, most notably in his ideas about farm life and the people who live it. But, while he has come to enjoy rural life, the fatal split he has between head and heart always prevents him from fully taking part in the life at Talbothays. Added to this are the attitudes he has absorbed in his home, probably unthinkingly, about such things as sexual behavior, which make it impossible for him to forgive Tess.

TESS OF THE D'URBERVILLES

CHAPTER 36-42

....

> **PHASE FIVE: CHAPTER THIRTY-SIX**

"Clare arose in the light of a dawn that was ashy and furtive, as though associated with crime." He sees the remnants of last night's meal still on the table, the extinguished fire-all the details that help to bring back the events of the night before. While he is in thought there comes a knock at the door. It is the neighboring cottager's wife, who is to do the housework while they are there. He tells her that she will not be needed, and he prepares breakfast. He calls Tess down. They are gentle with one another. She looks "absolutely pure. Nature, in her fantastic trickery, had set such a seal of maidenhood upon Tess's countenance that he gazed at her with a stupefied air." He begs her to tell him it is not true, but of course she cannot. He asks if "he" still lives. Tess thinks he means the baby, and tells him that the baby died. Then she understands that Angel is referring to "the man," and she says yes and that he is in England. At this, "a last despair passed over Clare's face." He then tells her, bitterly, that when he married her he knew he wasn't getting wealth or social standing, but he had thought he was getting innocence - but then he remembers he has vowed not to reproach her, and he ceases. Tess sees the situation completely from Angel's point of view, and realizes how much he has "lost." She says that she would never have let it go as far as marriage if she hadn't always known that there was a way out-divorce. He tells her that he cannot divorce her, even if she were publicly to admit her past. (Divorce in England at that time was extremely difficult and expensive.) She is shocked and says that she should have carried out her plan last night. What was that, he asks? To hang herself, she says. He is shaken by her works and sternly demands that she promise him that she will never attempt any such thing again. She gives her word, but assures him that she would have done it for his good. "However, to do it with my own hand is too good for me, after all. It is you, my poor ruined husband, who ought to strike the blow. I think I should love you more, if that were possible, if you could bring yourself to do it..." They grow silent and, breakfast over, he leaves to go to the mill, where he has decided to pursue his idea of learning milling, no matter what else has happened. He returns for lunch. When that meal is finished, Tess retires to the kitchen and busies herself there. Angel comes to her there and tells her not to work in the kitchen because she is not his servant but his wife. These words cause her to break into sobs which "would almost have won round any man but Angel Clare." But deep inside him there lies hidden "a hard logical deposit" which had "blocked his acceptance of the Church (and) it blocked his acceptance of Tess ... when he ceased to believe he ceased to follow." Angel remains hard and firm, and Tess drops into a life of wretchedness. Several of these misery-filled days pass and then Angel comes to a decision - they will have to separate. Tess agrees, as she agrees to everything he says. Several more days go by. Finally he tells her that he cannot live with her without despising himself and despising her as well. No matter where they might go, someone would be sure to turn up who knew about Tess and Alec, and when that happened their lives, and the lives of any children they might have, would be made miserable. Tess admits the force of this argument, although deep down she has hoped that if they were to remain together long enough, his determination might be broken down. She says that she will comply with his plan for separation by going home. So it is decided. That night they begin to pack their things, for both of them will be leaving Wellbridge Mill.

PHASE FIVE: CHAPTER THIRTY-SEVEN

Tess is awakened, about one o'clock in the morning, by a strange sound in the house. She sees the door of her bedroom open, and Angel enters. At first she is joyful, but her joy leaves her when she realizes he is sleep-walking. He comes to the middle of the room, stops, and murmurs, "in tones of indescribable sadness-'Dead! dead! dead!'" Tess remembers that he is liable to disturbances in his sleep when he is emotionally distressed (See Chapter Thirty-three), and so she is not alarmed. In any case, her love for him is so great that nothing he could do would frighten her. Angel approaches her bed and bends over her. He repeats "dead, dead, dead" again. Then he wraps her in the bedsheet like a shroud and lifts her from the bed "with as much respect as one would show to a dead body," and he carries her across the room murmuring "My poor, poor Tess - my dearest, darling Tess! So sweet, so good so true!" Tess is so happy to be in his arms that she makes no noise. He says, "My wife-dead, dead!" Then he kisses her on her lips - "lips in the daytime scorned." He descends the stairs, still holding Tess, and goes out into the night toward the river that runs nearby. Tess realizes that Angel is dreaming of that Sunday morning when he carried her through the water (see Chapter Twenty-three). They arrive at the river, at a place where the water is wide and deep. There is a narrow footbridge there, but the rail has been washed away and the plank is very slippery. He mounts this bridge and begins to walk across. Tess thinks he is going to drown her, and this thought makes her happy-at least she will have spent her last half-hour in her beloved Angel's arms. But he proceeds across, and they reach the other side safely. Here they are on the grounds of the old ruined abbey church. Against one of its walls is the row of tombs that mark the resting places of the abbots. Among these is an empty stone coffin, "in which every tourist with a turn for grim humour was accustomed to stretch himself." In this Angel carefully places Tess. He kisses her again, and then lies down on the ground alongside and falls into an exhausted sleep. Tess sits up in the coffin and looks about her. She realizes that Angel is only wearing his shirt and trousers and will certainly be chilled by the cool night air; she too is also clothed for bed and the sheet does not offer much protection from the cold. She tried to wake him but fails. Then it occurs to her to use persuasion. She says, "Let us walk on darling," and takes him by the arm. Her words apparently send him back into his dream, and he gets up and begins to walk back to the river. They cross the bridge and return to the house. She puts him to bed and goes to bed herself. In the morning - Tess sees that Angel is unaware of what went on during the night. In fact Angel has had, on awakening, an idea that something may have occurred during the night, but he knows that if the "something" vanishes in the light of day then it is only emotional and need not be reckoned with in making rational decisions. However, he remembers nothing of what went on, and so he proceeds with his plan of the day before-separation from Tess. Tess is tempted to tell him about his sleepwalking, but she decides against it. Angel has ordered a carriage, and they finish packing. Their route takes them by Talbothays, and they feel that must pay a visit there. Talbothays is different now: "the gold of the summer picture was now grey, the colours mean, the rich soil mud, and the river cold." Tess bravely bears the teasing of her friends, for she and Angel have agreed to make everything seem normal. She hears that Retty has gone home, and that Marian has left to look for work elsewhere Finally their visit is concluded, and they get back into their carriage. They drive until they come to the point where the roads fork, and where they must part if Tess is to go to Marlott. At this crossroads Angel tells her that he will let her know where he is as soon as he makes up his mind, and that he will come to her as soon as it is possible for him to do so. Until that time, however, he says, it will be better if she does not try to come to him. He also says that she may write to him if she is ill or in need. Tess agrees to all these conditions, only asking that he not make her "punishment ... more than I can bear." He gives her "a fairly good sum of money ... and they parted there and then." He gets out and watches the carriage with Tess in it, move off down the road. He gets a sudden hope that she will look back at him, but she is "lying in a half-dead faint inside." In this way they separate, and as Angel turns to take his road, he "hardly knew that he loved her still."

Comment

Angel's rejection of Tess, which occurred in the preceding chapter, was a conscious one, originating in that "hard logical deposit" that Hardy tells us lies deep down in Angel. In this chapter, however, it is Angel's unconscious mind that is at work.

Although Tess is rejected again here, there are important differences between this chapter and the one preceding. There Angel was hard and unyielding; here he is terribly sad and emotional. He treats Tess with the utmost of tenderness as he symbolically buries his wife in the open grave, signifying the end of his marriage. When he awakens he is not aware of the deep love he feels for Tess, and once again he is rational and unfeeling. (When he leaves Tess, he is hardly aware that he loved her still.) It is precisely this split between his emotions and his mind that allows Angel to do the heartless things he does to Tess. This opposition between heart and head, or between night and day, is one we have seen before in the book. Similarly, the change in the appearance of Talbothays is another example of the correspondence between the human events and the changes in nature that are present throughout Tess.

PHASE FIVE: CHAPTER THIRTY-EIGHT

Tess drives on until she reaches the turnpike gate of the highway that leads to Marlott. She asks the gateman (who is a new man and does not know her) for news of the village and is told about her wedding, and about how "Sir John" Durbeyfield celebrated the occasion. The information makes Tess sick at heart, and she decides not to drive into the village in the carriage but instead to leave her baggage at the driver's house and walk into Marlott by a back path. She makes her way to her parents' house and enters without her mother seeing her. Then Joan discovers her, and is astounded to find her there. In a burst of tears, Tess tells her everything. Mrs. Durbeyfield calls her a fool, and Tess pleads that she could not have deceived him. Mrs. Durbeyfield accepts the situation for want of anything better to do, but she is concerned about the effect the news will have on "Sir John." She tells Tess that he has been down at the tavern every day talking about his ancestry, and about the time when the d'Urbervilles will come back into their estates, etc. At that moment, Mr. Durbeyfield is heard approaching, and Tess's mother says that she will break the news herself. Tess goes upstairs to wait until her father is told, and while upstairs she sees that the beds had been shifted-

she realizes that there is no place for her now. Meanwhile, Jack Durbeyfield comes in and launches into an account of a discussion that had taken place down at Rolliver's tavern. Then he asks whether there had been any letter from Tess. His wife tells him that there has been no letter, but that Tess herself has come. And she proceeds to tell him all the details. His main concern is about what the fellows down at the tavern will say when they hear this after all the talking he has done. And then he asks his wife whether in fact Tess is married at all - "or is it like the first -" When Tess hears her word questioned by her father she knows she cannot remain at Marlott, and when, at the end of the week, a letter from Angel arrives telling her he has gone to the North of England to look at a farm, she uses this as an excuse to go. She tells her mother she is going to join him, and gives her mother twenty-five pounds, half the sum Angel has given her. Her mother now believes that Angel and Tess have come back together again.

PHASE FIVE: CHAPTER THIRTY-NINE

Three weeks have passed since his marriage, and Angel is now approaching his father's house in Emminster. During the time since he left Tess, he has tried to behave as if nothing has happened. He has continued mechanically to study agriculture, but inwardly he has been in a turmoil. He is bitter about the fact that he married Tess after he knew she was a d'Urberville. His principle of despising the old families was a correct one, and now that he has gone against it, he has been punished. He now is faced with reconstructing his entire life because all his former plans have involved Tess, and in a painfully intimate way. In traveling about from farm to farm he has noticed posters describing the opportunities available to immigrants in Brazil, and gradually the idea of Brazil implants itself in his mind. The season for traveling there is at hand, and he is strongly inclined to go, especially since he thinks that he and Tess might be able to make a new life there. It is to announce his plans for Brazil that he has come to Emminster. He has given no announcement of his visit, and his parents are very surprised to see him. They ask for Tess, and he tells them she is at her mother's. He tells them he is going to Brazil. They explain why they did not come to his wedding (it would have been inappropriate and embarrassing to everyone concerned), and they tell him they are looking forward to meeting his wife. He describes her to his mother, and she is pleased with what she hears. Mr. Clare says that since Angel is here he will read a different Biblical passage than the one he had planned to read in his daily prayers. He chooses the thirty-first chapter of the Book of Proverbs, which is a praise of a virtuous wife. His mother says, "Since she is pure and chaste she would have been refined enough for me." The chapter from Proverbs and his mother's words burn like fire into Angel's heart, and he leaves the parlor as soon as he can. His mother follows him. She feels, with a mother's instinct, that there is something wrong between her son and his wife. She asks if they have quarreled. No, not exactly, he replies. "Angel-is she a young woman whose history will bear investigation? "'She is spotless!' he replied; and felt that if it had sent him to eternal hell there and then he would have told that lie." His mother says that nothing else matters; Tess can learn all the social graces she may not now possess. Angel realizes that his marriage has also wrecked his career; he has not been overly concerned about it, but he had wished to do well if only for his family. He sees himself as a complete failure, and he grows angry at Tess for putting him in a situation that requires him to deceive his parents.

Comment

Hardy comments that over Tess and Angel hangs the greatest difficulty of all-Angel's limitations. For all his advanced thinking, and for all his high morality and good intentions, he is still, deep in his heart, "the slave to custom and conventionality when surprised back into his early teachings." And, obviously, the blow he has received from Tess has turned him back to those early, conventional teachings. Because of his limitations he cannot see that Tess is that woman of which the Book of Proverbs speaks: one whose "price is far above rubies." "In considering what Tess was not, he overlooked what she was, and forgot that the defective can be more than the entire." It should always be remembered that the subtitle of *Tess of the d'Urbervilles* is "A Pure Woman Faithfully Represented."

PHASE FIVE: CHAPTER FORTY

At breakfast the Clare family talks of Brazil and of the wonderful things that are to be had there, despite the fact that some laborers had been to Brazil in the last year and had returned, discouraged, within a year. After breakfast Angel goes into town to draw out his money from the bank, and there meets Miss Mercy Chant. She has heard that he is going to leave England and says that she imagines Brazil will be very profitable for Angel. He admits that it may indeed be, but he is disturbed by the break that leaving England will make in his life. He remarks, "Perhaps a cloister would be preferable." Being the strict Protestant that she is, she is scandalized at the mention of "cloister," because it implies monks and Roman Catholicism. Angel's nerves are stretched to the breaking point, and Mercy's small-mined prejudices make him do something he would never ordinarily dream of doing-he whispers to her the most shockingly unorthodox ideas he can think of. She is horrified, and he must excuse himself as best he can: "I think I am going crazy." They part on this note, and Angel deposits an additional thirty pounds at his bank to be sent to Tess. This along with the fifty pounds he has given her should suffice, especially since she has been told to go to his father in the event of an emergency.

The last obligation he must fulfill before leaving for Brazil is to go back to Wellbridge Mill, in order to give up the key and pay the small rent for the time he and Tess had been there. He enters the farmhouse while the farmer is in the fields, and the sight of the rooms brings back the memories of his "honeymoon" with a rush. As he sees all the small things that bring back Tess's image to his mind, for the first time there passes through his mind the thought that he may have acted unwisely, harshly. Tears come to his eyes and he says, "O Tess! If you had only told me sooner, I would have forgiven you!" Hearing someone come in, he goes to the stairs and sees a face he knows-Izz Huett, from Talbothays. She says that she has called to see him and Tess, for she had an idea that they would be returning to Wellbridge. He tells her why he has come, and asks if he can give her a ride to wherever she might be going. After he settles his debt with the farmer, Izz jumps up on his gig and they drive together. He tells her he is leaving for Brazil to see what life is like there, and after he has set himself up he will send for Tess. He asks about Retty and Marian, and learns that Retty is ill with a disease that no one can diagnose-she seems to be wasting away-while Marian has become a drunkard. Izz says she is all right, but that she too has seen happier times. Angel asks why, and her look indicates clearly that it is because she still loves him. She admits it, and he is astonished. They approach a turning and Izz says that she must get off here. Angel slows down. He feels angry at social **conventions** because he feels they have ruined his life. He decides to take revenge on society by breaking all its rules. He therefore tells Izz that he is going to Brazil because he is separated from

Tess for personal reasons and may never live with her again. "I may not be able to love you; but-will you go with me instead of her?" She asks whether he truly wants her to go, and he says he does. After some thought she says she will go. He asks her whether she understands the conditions, and she says that she does, but that being with him would make up for all of them. He tells her not to get out but to stay in the gig, and they drive on. He asks her again whether she loves him very much and she says that she has loved him ever since she met him at the dairy. Does she love him more than Tess? "No, not more than she." "How's that?" "Because nobody could love 'ee more than Tess did! ... She would have laid down her life for 'ee. I could do no more." Her last words echo in his ears, and suddenly he tells her that he hasn't known what he has been saying. She is to forget everything that he has said that day. Izz is heart-broken and bursts into tears. Gradually she calms down as they drive back toward her turning. He asks her to forgive his "momentary levity." "Forget it? Never, never! O, it was no levity to me!" Izz, however, is a generous girl and, seeing that Angel is genuinely sorry for what he has done, forgives him and they part on good terms. He tells her that her words have saved him from betraying his wife, and with that he leaves her. Izz is miserable and so is Angel. He is on the point of turning off the road that led to the railroad station and instead going to Tess. But he checks his impulse because he realizes that, despite Tess's love as reinforced by Izz's words, the facts have not changed. If he was right then, he is right now. That night he takes the train for London, and five days later is saying good-bye to his brothers at the ship.

Comment

Mercy Chant is another in the series of portraits Hardy gives us of religious persons in this book, and like all of them she is not admirable. She glories in misfortune (because it only shows that the Lord is unhappy with sinful man) and is insistent on those doctrines that divide her religion from that of others. "I glory in my Protestantism," she says. She is humorless and passionless, except in questions of theology. She is sterile and narrow-minded, and has no use for any life except that led according to her principles.

Angel's limitations, so clearly seen in his behavior toward Tess, show themselves again in the way he acts to Izz. It is meaningless to attempt to revenge oneself on society, and certainly Angel's irresponsible actions with regard to Izz's feelings are foolish and immature in the extreme.

PHASE FIVE: CHAPTER FORTY-ONE

It is now the October following the parting of Tess and Angel. Tess, during the summer, has worked at a dairy that is distant from both Marlott and Talbothays. She has been in a period of stagnation, mentally speaking, her mind being "at that other dairy, at that other season," with Angel. She finds work through the harvest season, and thus has not had to dip into the money that Angel left or her. Then, however, there came a period of wet weather, which prevented her from working, and she has to begin to spend the twenty-five pounds that remains to her. When this money was nearly gone she received a letter from her mother telling her that the rains had gone through the thatched roof, and that the Durbeyfield family literally did not have a roof over its heads. Could she not send the twenty pounds that they needed? Tess has thirty pounds coming to her from Angel's bank, and she sends twenty to her mother. Part of the rest she must spend for winter clothing, and so she finds herself facing the long winter with only a small sum in her pocket. She knows that she can call upon Angel's parents in the event of an emergency, but her pride makes this thought extremely unpleasant. If she is hesitant to approach her husband's parents, she is completely set against telling her own parents the truth about her circumstances. She is perfectly content to have them think that Angel has gone to set up a home for them in Brazil, and that she will follow him as soon as possible. Meanwhile Angel is ill of fever in Brazil, and the situation there for Englishmen is one of misery. Apparently all the promises to the emigrants were only words, and the newcomers are struggling to keep alive. In England, Tess has just spent the last of her money, and she searches about for work. She knows that she would be taken back at Talbothays, if only out of pity, but she cannot bear the thought of all the gossip that would circulate at her expense. She is now on her way to a farm which she has heard of in a letter from Marian. Marian has learned that Tess is separated from Angel, and she has notified Tess that there is work to be had if she is interested. Tess now finds herself in a difficult situation because her beauty attracts unwelcome attention. As she tramps along the road leading to the farm that is her destination, she is overtaken by a man who says hello to her. It is twilight, and by the remaining light the man asks whether she isn't "young squire d'Urberville's friend." He is the man who had recognized her at the inn the previous Christmas and had fought with Angel because of what he said at that time. She doesn't answer him. He tells her that she should beg his pardon for the blow he got from Angel that night. She feels trapped, and suddenly she begins to run. She darts down the road and then ducks into a grove of trees. She rushes into this wood until she is sure that she is safe from discovery. There she makes a bed for herself in the dry leaves and falls asleep. Her sleep is restless. She dreams of Angel comfortable in a warm climate while she is chilly and cold. Mixed in with these dreams are strange noises: "sometimes it was a palpitation, sometimes a flutter; sometimes it was a sort of gasp or gurgle." She is sure that the noises are being made by some wild creature but she is not alarmed: "outside humanity, she had … no fear." At daybreak she awakens and explores the place in which she has spent the night. Immediately she understands that the noises were and what had caused them. She sees several peasants lying on the ground, some wounded, some dead. She realizes that the birds had been driven into this wood by a hunting party the day before. The birds that had been killed had been carried off by the shooters, but many wounded birds had taken refuge in the trees, and as they weakened had fallen to the ground, thus making the noises she had heard. Tess remembers having seen hunters when she was a girl and having been frightened by the "blood-thirsty light in their eyes." Tess, "with the impulse of a soul who could feel for kindred sufferers as much as for herself," puts the wounded pheasants out of their misery by wringing their necks. She feels ashamed of herself for having thought of herself as miserable when the pheasants were in true misery.

Comment

It is again October, and the decline in Tess's fortunes that corresponds with the decline of the year (which we have come to expect) again takes place. We might ask why Tess does not try to get work in town and thus be free from dependence on seasonal farm work. Hardy answers that she fears towns and town life and manners because she has had no experience in anything but a rural environment and also because all her hardships have come from persons of "gentility," persons who have been educated and have had all the "advantages" of modern civilization. Quite in line with her distaste for urban life is her fearlessness in "her" world, the world of the fields. Significant here is her identification with the slaughtered birds because the hunted, beautiful pheasants are in the same position that she is. (She has already been compared to a bird in a trap earlier, in Chapter Thirty-one). Hardy repeats that Tess feels condemned "under an arbitrary law of society which had no foundation in Nature." Again and again Hardy strives to show that the ways men regulate their lives are "unnatural" in the sense that they have nothing to do with, and are usually in opposition to, the great system of Nature of which men are a part. Humans come to disaster precisely because they attempt to go against Nature and of course cannot contend with it, they being so puny and it being so vast.

PHASE FIVE: CHAPTER FORTY-TWO

She sets out again in the morning, strengthened by the thought that her suffering, compared to that of the pheasants, is really not so intolerable as she had thought. She comes to the town of Chalk-Newton, where she has breakfast, and where she again attracts attention because of her beauty. She decides to do something about her appearance. She therefore dresses herself in her oldest field-gown, wraps a handkerchief around her face, and snips off her eyebrows. She trudges on all that day and all the next, all the while looking for word. First she seeks work she likes best, like dairy and poultry work, and ends with activities she least desired because they were hardest and heaviest-field labor. However, there is nothing to be found, and it seems as if she will have to go on to Marian's farm, which she had been keeping as a last resort because it involves hard, heavy labor. Towards the evening of the second day she reaches the plateau that lies between the valley in which Marlott is located and that in which Talbothays is situated. Here the land is dry, dusty, cold, and hard. The landscape seems unfriendly and stubborn, but there seems no escaping the fact that she will have to spend the winter here, for all else has failed her. She has come to Flintcomb-

Ash, the farm on which Marian has been working. Tess enters the tiny village near the farm and looks for Marian, whom she soon finds. Marian is struck by Tess's sad appearance, and she cannot understand how or why Tess should have been reduced to such a life. Tess asks Marian to oblige her and not ask too many questions. Marian complies. Tee inquires whether there is any work available and Marian says there is because the work is so hard that few care to do it. Flintcomb-Ash is a "starve-acre place," she says. The only crops are "corn and swedes" (wheat and turnips), and Marian tells her she will be set to "awede-hacking" (weeding and harvesting turnips, back-breaking work). Tess is willing, but tells Marian not to mention a word of her past-she doesn't want Angel's name to be besmirched. The farmer not being there, Tess is hired by the farmer's wife, and she engages herself to stay all winter, until Old Lady-Day (April 6). She writes to her parents to give them her new address but she does not tell them of her circumstances.

Comment

Flintcomb-Ash is the scene of the action for most of the remainder of the book, and its physical appearance is symbolic of the decline that is taking place in Tess's life. Talbothays was lush, moist, and fertile, and its inhabitants were friendly; Flintcomb-Ash, as its name implies, is flinty in its hardness, dry as ashes, sterile, and its people (as we shall soon see) are unfriendly. Tess spends the bountiful summer at the dairy, the barren winter at the turnip farm. Talbothays is in a rich valley, Flintcomb is on a bare plateau. The dairy teems with life; Flintcomb is a "starve-acre place."

TESS OF THE D'URBERVILLES

. . . .

PHASE FIVE: CHAPTER FORTY-THREE

Tess is set to work in the swede-field. The upper half of the turnip has already been eaten by the livestock, and Tess and Marian must hack out the root so that it too may be consumed. The earth is bare and lifeless, like "a face ... without features," and the sky above is similarly empty. Under the white sky the two girls "crawl over the surface [of the earth] like flies." They work on in all kinds of weather, for while they can stop when it rains, if they do they will not be paid. Yet even when they are wet through and through, they are sustained by their memories of Talbothays. Sometimes, when they are not swede-hacking, they are engaged at swede-trimming, in which they slice off the earth and fibers from the turnips before storing them. When they do this work, they can shelter themselves in a small hut if it rains, but the work continues long and hard. Through it all, they keep returning to that wonderful summer at the dairy, talking about it endlessly. Then Marian gets the idea that Flintcomb would be a more bearable place to stay the winter if they could bring in a few others from the old Talbothays days. She decides to write Izz, who replies that she will come if she can. The winter gets progressively worse. The few trees and bushes take on a coating of damp frost, soon followed by a time of dry frost. The latter is accompanied by strange visitors: "birds from behind the North Pole began to arrive silently ... gaunt spectral creatures with tragical eyes - eyes which had witnessed scenes of cataclysmal horror in inaccessible polar regions of a magnitude such as no human being had even conceived." After the frost and the birds comes a peculiarly bonechilling cold, followed by snow. The field work is halted, and the two girls join the rest of the women at reed-drawing, which is even harder than working in the swede-field. (Reed-drawing involves pulling the straw from sheaves of wheat). When they enter the barn, they are delighted to see Izz, who is working side by side with two other women. Tess is startled to recognize them as Car Darch and her sister, from Trantridge, but they do not remember her. After several hours of silent work (the girls cannot talk freely because of the presence of Car and her sister), the farmer comes in. Tess, who has not yet met him, is dismayed to find that he is none other than the native of Trantridge from whom she had fled that night on the road and who had been in the fight with Angel at the inn. He knows he has Tess in his power and he demands that she beg his pardon. She refuses, but she knows that the farmer will take every opportunity to make things hard for her. Tess is inexperienced at reed-drawing and thus accomplishes much less than the other four, who are old hands. The farmer (who is named Groby) insists that she do her share. Tess says that in order to get the work done she will stay on all afternoon, instead of quitting at two o'clock like the others. At two, the sisters from Trantridge leave, and Marian and Izz volunteer to help Tess. Now they can talk, and inevitably they reminisce about Talbothays and their love for Angel. Tess says that she cannot take part in their talk of Angel because, despite her present circumstances, she still is Mrs. Angel Clare and cannot speak of him as they do. Izz is not impressed by her defense of Angel: "I don't think he is a too fond husband to go away from you so soon." Tess tries to defend him, her voice choked with tears. Their talk stops and they continue working. Suddenly Tess feels weak and sinks down on the straw to rest. Izz and Marian tell her to lie down and that they will finish her work. She hears them whispering between themselves, and she is sure that they are talking about Angel. Tess wants very much to hear what they are saying. She persuades herself that her fatigue has passed, and she goes to rejoin them. At this point Izz, who the night before had walked twelve miles to get to Flintcomb and who has had very little sleep, is overcome by tiredness. Tess thanks her for helping and tells her not to do any more. Izz leaves. Marian, who has been sustained by the bottle of liquor that she always carries, is now somewhat dreamy and confiding. Without thinking what its effect on Tess will be, she tells Tess what Izz has told her - Angel's offer to take her to Brazil. Tess bursts into tears and Marian is sorry she has told her. But Tess says she is glad she has found out because it shows that she has been negligent in writing to him. She decides to write and not wait until he sends a letter. That night she starts to write a letter to Angel, but she is beset by doubts and is unable to finish it. How can she plead the hardship of her life to one who proposed to run off with Izz so shortly after leaving her?

Comment

The passage in which the two girls are described as flies crawling over the hostile earth and under a hostile sky brings to mind a similar sentiment from Shakespeare's *King Lear*: "As flies to wanton boys are we to the gods; They kill us for their sport" (Act IV, scene 1, 36-37). The ghastliness and despair evoked by the image of the featureless faces of heaven and earth are reinforced by the horrible birds that come as heralds of disaster. Added to this dismal scene is the terrible winter, which is more severe than any in recent years. Through this mass of detail Hardy is not only alerting the reader to the downfall that Tess is to undergo, but is also making Nature a character in the novel. That is, Nature is present in many novels as a backdrop, the scenery or setting against which events take place. Here, however, Nature is more than that. Nature is active, Nature seems to be taking a hand in bringing about Tess's misfortunes. Again the similarity to *King Lear* comes to mind, for in that work, too, the forces of Nature enter into the world of the action in much the same way that a human character would.

PHASE FIVE: CHAPTER FORTY-FOUR

Marian's words about Angel and Izz turn Tess's thoughts to Angel's family in Emminster. She has often thought about them but has felt that she had no claim on them. But now she feels that she has been driven too far. Why hasn't Angel written to her? Is he ill? Or is he not interested enough to write? She thinks to herself that if Angel's father is truly the good man she has been told he is, then he will be sympathetic to her situation; moreover, he may have had word of Angel. She decides to go to Emminster, but the only day she can leave Flintcomb is Sunday. There being no railroad, she must walk. She leaves two weeks later, at four o'clock on a crisp Sunday morning. It is now a day less than a year since her marriage. The road is deserted, she makes good time. But as she gets closer to Emminster her confidence begins with wane. She arrives about noon and taking off her thick walking boots, stuffs them into a hedge where she can find them; then she puts on thin, pretty shoes for her appearance in the Clare household. She comes to the door, gathers up all her courage, and rings the bell. No one answers. A second ring, and again no answer. Then she realizes that they are all in church and will be arriving soon. Not wishing to call attention to herself, she decides not to wait but to return when the family has come home. She begins to walk away and moves past the church. The services are just over, and she is swept up in the crowd exiting from the church. She does not like the stares she is receiving and decides therefore to walk to the outskirts of the town until the Clare family will have finished eating. She rapidly outdistances all the townspeople except two young men who are walking behind her. As they approach, she cannot help but recognize the similarities between their voices and that of Angel. She realizes that they are his two brothers, out for a stroll before dinner. Only one of the townspeople, a somewhat stiff-looking young woman, is in front of Tess. Angel's brothers see her and one says, "There is Mercy Chant. Let us overtake her." The sight of Mercy causes one of the Clare brothers to say that he will always regret Angel's hasty and ill-considered marriage. To think that he could have married a fine ladylike person like Mercy Chant and instead threw himself away on a milkmaid! The brothers pass Tess and greet Mercy. As they talk together one of the brothers probes about in the hedge with his umbrella and uncovers Tess's boots. The three surmise that the boots must have been left there by a beggar who is going barefoot to gain sympathy. Mercy picks them up and takes them with her. She says she will give them to a poor deserving person, and the three of them walk back to the Clare house and go inside. Tess is in tears. She knows that it is senseless, but she cannot help but feel that the Clare family has condemned her. She does not have the emotional strength to return to the house, and she turns away and begins the long walk back to Flintcomb. Tess cannot know that she has made an error in thinking that Mr. Clare would feel about her as his sons do. Her return trip is dreary and tedious. She is depressed by the fact that she now must stay at Flintcomb until she gets enough courage to try again at Emminster; besides that, she is walking in thin shoes that were not meant for long hikes. She does not pass a house for eight miles and finally comes to the village where she had eaten breakfast that morning. She again stops there for some refreshment. As she eats, she asks a woman who is a native of the place where everyone is, for the town seems deserted. The woman tells her that the entire population has gone to hear "the preaching in yonder barn." There "a ranter" holds forth in a religious revival meeting. After Tess has finished her small meal, she proceeds on her way through the village, and as she passes the barn she hears the voice of the rant r. The sermon is centered on "justification by faith," the doctrine that holds that the moral law is of no importance compared with the quality of the faith of the believer. Tess is struck by the similarity of the sermon to the beliefs of Angel's father, and she stops outside to hear a bit of it. To support what he has been saying the preacher begins to relate some of his personal experiences. He says that he had been the greatest of sinners until the day of awakening came. Then, when God's word had sunk into his heart, his life changed completely overnight. But more striking to Tess than the doctrine she hears is the voice in which the words are being uttered. It seems to her, impossible enough, to be the voice of Alec d'Urberville. She comes around to the front of the barn and looks in. The audience is made up entirely of villagers, including the man with the pot of red paint whom she has met before. And indeed, there speaking to this crowd, is none other than her seducer.

Comment

In this chapter we see still another piece of bad luck for Tess. It is unfortunate that she comes upon the sons instead of the father as she waits outside the house in Emminster. For all his gloomy theology, Angel's father would certainly have sympathized with Tess and helped her; he, unlike his two oldest sons, possesses human feeling and does not, as they do, take the outward appearance for the inner reality. It is bitterly ironic that while Tess does not get to see Angel's father, she does get to see one of his converts-Alec d'Urberville. The reintroduction of Alec marks the beginning of the next-to-last phase in Tess's sad life. Phase Five is called "Two Woman Pays," because in it Tess "pays" by leading a very hard life, both materially and emotionally. In Phase Six, Tess will begin to "pay" in a different way, that is, spiritually, and so it is proper that the appearance of Alec should close a section of the novel.

PHASE SIX ("THE CONVERT"): CHAPTER FORTY-FIVE

Since Tess has neither seen nor heard from Alec since she left Trantridge, she stares in disbelief at the man in front of her. His dandyish dress has changed to a version of minister's clothing. His handsome and sensual face is still passionate, but the passion now is spiritual and godly. His former energy and dash are still present, but they have been put to the service of religion: "animalism had become fanaticism." As soon as she grasps the changes that have come over him, her impulse is to flee. But as she turns to go he sees her. As he does, "his fire … seems to go out of him." The shock has been as great to him as it was to her, and his eloquence falters. In that moment she recovers and starts walking as fast as she can. The sight of him makes her despair because it forcefully demonstrates that her hope for a new life completely divorced from her past is without foundation. The appearance of Alec stands as a powerful reminder of an "implacable past." The past would never be completely paid for until she was a part of it, until she was dead. As she is absorbed in these thoughts, she becomes aware of footsteps behind her. It is Alec, "the one personage in all the world she wished not to encounter alone on this side of the grave." He is excited by the feelings within him, feelings called into being by the sight of Tess. She answers his greeting coldly. He tells her that he has come after her because he feels that it is his duty and his desire to try to save her from God's wrath. She asks whether he has succeeded in saving himself. In reply he says that he has been saved through the action of Reverend James Clare. He tells her of his encounter with Angel's father (of which we learned earlier) and how he insulted him. The minister told him at that time that "those who come to scoff sometimes remain to pray." These words sank into Alec's mind, but it was not until his mother died that "he began to see daylight." Since that time he has been engaged in sharing and spreading this light. Tess's response to Alec's words is one of passionate anger: "I can't believe in such sudden things!... You, and those like you, take your fill of pleasure on earth by making the life of such as me bitter and black with sorrow; and then it is a fine thing, when you have enough of that, to think of securing your pleasure in heaven by becoming converted!" She goes on to say that she cannot believe in his religion because a better man than he (i.e., Angel) does not believe in it. She thinks that Alec may be sincere at the moment, but she also thinks his religious feeling is only a flash, and "such flashes as you feel, Alec, I fear don't last!" With these words she turns and faces him. He is disturbed by her look, and says: "Don't look at me like that!" She is flustered and turns away: "And there was revived in her the wretched sentiment which had often come to her before, that in inhabiting the fleshly tabernacle [the physical body] with which Nature had endowed her she was somehow doing wrong." He tells her that she should wear a veil over her good looks because her beautiful face has a power over him which he would like to forget. After this their conversation becomes casual and they walk on. She wonders how far he will accompany her. Finally they come to a place called "Cross-in-Hand." This is the most deserted spot in the desolate landscape. It gets its name from a stone pillar upon which is carved a human hand. Its origin is unknown, and it is said to have a "sinister" quality. At Cross-in-Hand Alec tells Tess he must leave her, for his path lies in a direction different than hers. As they are about to part, he remarks that she speaks better English than she did when he last saw her, and asks where she has learned it. "I have learnt many things in my troubles," she replies. Alec asks what troubles she has had, and Tess tells him of the baby and its death, the only one of her troubles that concerns him. D'Urberville had not known anything of this, and he asks why she never let him know. She doesn't answer, and he says, "Well-you will see me again." She tells him not to come near her. He admits that seeing her has shaken him, and he says that he fears her. In order to lessen his fear, he asks her to put her hand upon the stone hand on the cross and swear that she will never tempt him. She exclaims that such a thing is the furthest from her mind, but he demands that she do it. Tess is frightened and swears on the strange cross. Alec leaves Tess and starts out across the plateau to his preaching engagement. As he walks, he reads a letter he carries. It is from Reverend James Clare. In it he expresses his pleasure at Alec's conversion and his interest in helping Alec in any plans he may have as a preacher. Alec reads and rereads this letter until he calms down and the image of Tess leaves his mind. Tess, meanwhile, walks along until she meets a shepherd. She asks him about Cross-in-Hand, and whether it was an ever a holy cross. The shepherd replies that it never was holy at all. Instead, it was put up by the relatives of an evildoer in the old times who was first tortured there by nailing his hand to a post and was afterwards hanged. "'Tis a thing of ill omen, Miss....

They say he sold his soul to the devil, and that he walks at times." Tess is horrified by this information and continues to walk. As she approaches Flintcomb-Ash she sees a girl and her lover without their observing her. As she comes closer, she recognizes the girl as Izz. When Tess is evasive about the results of her trip to Emminster, Izz tells her that the young man is named Amby Seedling, and is from Talbothays. He found out that she was at Flintcomb and followed her here to ask her to marry him. He has confessed that he has been in love with her for two years, but she tells Tess that she has "hardly answered him."

Comment

Hardy gives us several indications that Alec's religion is not very deeply planted in him, and thus we will not be surprised when he later loses his faith nearly as fact as he found it. (That change does not mean, however, that Alec is insincere in his belief at this point in the story.) The oath he makes Tess swear is an indication of what is to come. It is a ghastly mockery of a true oath because it is taken on a "devil's cross." Also Alec cannot suppress his natural sensuality when he looks at Tess. Hardy is implying that there is a definite connection between sensuality and the kind of religion that Alec preaches: "the lipshapes that had meant seductiveness were now made to express supplication; the glow on the cheek that yesterday could be translated as riotousness was evangelized to-day into the splendours of pious rhetoric; ... the bold rolling eye that had flashed upon her form in the old time with such mastery now beamed with the rude energy of theolatry [worship of God] that was almost ferocious." The portrait of the "new" Alec completes the gallery that Hardy has drawn of religious persons in this book. As has been said before, all the religious persons in this book. As has been said before, all the religious persons are limited and distorted to some extent in that their devotion blinds them to some aspect of life. Notice that the only religious person for whom Hardy has a good word is Angel's father, and in him it is the human rather than the theological that Hardy commends. (For a further discussion of Hardy's views on religion, see the Essay Questions.)

The appearance of Izz's lover from Talbothays is a further piece of **irony**. He arrives just when Tess has been rejected by the family of her husband, who also was her lover at Talbothays.

Cross-in Hand has a further significance for Tess. It means that from this point on she has taken her cross in hand, as Christ took His, and that her progress henceforth will be to her personal Calvary - a hill in the town of Wintoncester (see Chapter Fifty-nine). Each of the fourteen chapters from this point to her death contains some difficult trial, and may be seen as corresponding to the fourteen Stations of the Cross. It is no accident that the last phase of the novel is entitled "Fulfillment," for in Tess fulfills her destiny as Christ did His.

PHASE SIX: CHAPTER FORTY-SIX

It is several days later. Tess is working out in the field, feeding turnips into the slicing machine. Alec appears, much to Tess's distress. He tells her that now that his mother is dead he intends to sell the house and go off to Africa as a missionary. He has come to ask her to go with him as his wife. Startled, she replies that she cannot. He asks whether she is sure and she says there is no possibility of her changing her mind. She says that she loves someone else. He cannot believe it, and she is forced to admit that she is married. She regrets having told him, begs him to keep her secret. He asks who her husband is; she refuses to tell.

Alec observes that he cannot be much of a husband, whoever he is, if he has left Tess alone like this. Tess is very disturbed by the conversation and begs him to leave. He agrees and is about to go when Farmer Groby comes up to find out what they are doing. Alec is angered by Groby's crude questions and it appears that a fight may be brewing, but then Alec decides to go. As Groby reprimands Tess, she thinks momentarily of Alec's offer of marriage. Were she free to accept, all the hardships she suffers would be eliminated. "But no, no! I could not have married him now! He is so unpleasant to me." That night she starts another letter to Angel telling him of her love and hiding her present difficulties, yet between the lines there is "some monstrous fear-almost a desperation." But she doesn't finish this letter, and she doesn't send it.

It is now February 2, the day of the Candlemas Fair. All the laborers go to this fair because it is there that new engagements are made for the next year. Tess is one of the few who doesn't go because she had "a vaguely shaped hope that something would happen to render another outdoor engagement unnecessary." She has just finished her dinner when she sees Alec outside her door. His appearance is somehow different. He enters and immediately bursts out: "Tess-I couldn't help it! ... now I cannot get rid of your image, try how I may!" He begs her to pray for him. She asks how she can pray for him when she doesn't believe that God would answer her prayers. She says that she has been "cured of the presumption of thinking otherwise." Alec asks who has taught her this, and Tess says that it was her husband. Alec concludes that she has no religion, perhaps as a result of what he had done to her. Tess disagrees. She says she has a religion, but she doesn't believe in a supernatural power that governs all. Alec then says "uneasily" that he is certain about his own faith. Tess says that she believes in the "spirit of the Sermon on the Mount, and so did my dear husband," but she does not believe in anything more than that. Alec chides her for blindly accepting everything her husband said, but she denies the charge. She says that he simply "knew everything" and therefore never had to force her to agree. She came to see everything from his point of view because he, who had thought about these matters so long and hard, was much more likely to be right than she, who had never thought of them at all. Alec asks her what he used to say. Tess's keen memory brings back one of Angel's "merciless syllogisms" [chains of reasoning] on this subject, and she delivers it perfectly, even imitating his accent and manner. Alec asks her to repeat it, and she does. "Anything else?" he asks. Tess proceeds to repeat another of Angel's arguments. She admits she doesn't understand this last one, "but I know it is right." Alec falls into thought. He asks her whether her husband knew that she was "as big an infidel as he." She says she never told him. Alec says that she is better off than he is because he is now tortured by doubts arising from what she has told him. He tells her that he came all the way to Flintcomb to see her, although he had started out to go to the Fair, where he has a preaching engagement. Tess says he will never make it in time now, and he replies that he knows that but doesn't care. He says he is not going to preach because of his desire to see her - a woman he once despised. He retracts this statement, saying that he never really despised her because she was the one girl who remained pure despite her "fall." "You withdrew yourself from me so quickly and resolutely when you saw the situation; you did not remain at my pleasure: so there was one petticoat in the world for whom I had no contempt, and you are she." She is horrified at his words: "O Alec ... what have I done?" She has been, he tells her, the innocent means through which he lost his faith. Since she has come back into his life he has not been able to hold fast to his belief. Her image has been in his mind night and day. He has been filled with a desire to help her, protect her, especially since learning that she has been deserted by her husband. Tess beseeches him to leave her and not speak against her absent husband. He agrees to go but he realizes that he is finished with preaching. He swears that he will keep away from her, but he is not sure he can hold to his vow. He asks for one farewell kiss. Tess begs him not to force her. He tears himself away: "his eyes were equally barren of worldly and religious faith. The corpses of those old fitful passions which had lain inanimate amid the lines of his face ever since his reformation seemed to wake and come together as in a resurrection. He leaves, but Angel's words, as relayed through Tess, continue to work on him. He comes to find his position untenable. His enthusiasm is chilled and his faith drops away. As he thinks again and again of what Tess has told him he says to himself that Angel little thought, when he told her those things, that "he might be paving my way back to her!"

Comment

It is bitterly ironic that, as Alec says, Angel's own words, through Tess's innocent mouth, should be the means of her final ruin. Perhaps even more ironic is the fact that it is the wild, immoral, unprincipled Alec who has seen from the very first that Tess, despite her experience with him is still as pure as she ever was. The highly "moral" Angel is incapable of perceiving this until it is too late.

PHASE SIX: CHAPTER FORTY-SEVEN

It is now March, the time of the threshing of the last wheat rick. (A rick is a pile of wheat, protected from the rain by thatching.) Farmer Groby wants, if possible, to have the job finished that day, so the work is to begin at dawn. When Tess and Izz arrive at the rick, they see the "red tyrant" they have "come to serve" - the threshing machine which, whilst it was going, kept up a despotic demand upon the endurance of their muscles and nerves." A little way from the machine stood the engine which supplied the power for the thresher, and next to it stood the engineman. He travels with his engine and thresher from farm to farm and has absolutely no concern with or interest in the farms he works on; he cares about nothing but his machines. The thatch is stripped off the rick, and all the laborers take their places in the chain that leads from the top of the stack to the threshing machine. It continues from there to the straw rick, on which is piled the straw that results from the threshing. Groby orders Tess to take a particularly difficult place in the line: she is to stand on the platform of the machine, close to the man who feeds it, her job being to untie each sheaf of grain that is handed to her so that the feeder can place it in the machine. The reason Tess's job is difficult is that, while those on the grain pile or the straw pile can rest a bit or talk from time to time, those on the machine can never stop because the machine never stops. In addition, they are continually assailed by the noise, heat, and vibration of the thresher. The work continues straight through the day, the workers eating their meals right at the rick to save time. Because Tess is being deafened by the din of the machine, and is unable to turn away from it, she is not aware that a man has come silently into the field and has been standing to one side and watching her. He is dressed in a fashionable tweed suit, and he twirls a walking stick. Izz notices him and asks Marian who he is. Marian supposes that he is the lover of one of the women. Izz thinks he is after Tess, but Marian says that the man who has been pursuing Tess is a Methodist parson, not a dandy like this one. Izz remarks that they are the same man, only that this one is well dressed and has shaved off his beard. Marian says that he ought to leave Tess alone, she being a married woman.

Izz replies that there is no chance of his making any headway with her because she is so much in love with Angel. When dinnertime comes, Tess has been so shaken by the continual noise and vibration of the machine that she can hardly walk. She suddenly notices the "gentleman," and she decides to eat her meal alone on the rick. (There being a sharp wind blowing, all the others descend and lunch under the shelter of the stack.) She begins to eat. Alec, for he is the "gentleman," climbs the ladder and sits down next to her. He tells her that ever since she told him of their child his feelings, which had been "flowing in a strong puritanical stream, had suddenly found a way open in the direction of you, and had all at once gushed through. The religious channel is left dry forthwith; and it is you who have done it!" He tells her that he has given up all preaching engagements, and he makes fun of his audiences, "the brethren." But he doesn't care. It would be pure hypocrisy to continue preaching when his faith is gone. He tells her that since he last saw her he has been thinking about what her husband said and he has come to realize that he was right. He cannot understand how he was fired by Reverend Clare's faith. Equally, he cannot understand how Angel and Tess have come to hold a system of ethics without any belief in a supernatural power. She tries to show him that it is quite possible to have such a belief, but her lack of training and her basically emotional nature prevent her from arguing well enough to persuade him. Alec has lost his faith and he is glad of it because he can now once again be with Tess, who is more beautiful than ever. Her mouth is dry and she can barely eat as she realizes that she now has to contend with Alec once more, and that he will not easily be put off. He once again chides Tess about her absent husband, and the tears come to her eyes. He then comes to the point: it is to make his offer again-to invite her to go off with him, only this time not as his wife and not to Africa as a missionary. Tess picks up one of her heavy leather gloves and slaps him across the face with it. His mouth begins to bleed, and she is desperate. She looks at him "with the hopeless defiance of the sparrow's gaze before its captor twists its neck. 'Whip me, crush me; you need not mind those people under the rick! I shall not cry out. Once victim, always victim - that's the law!'" Alec replies coolly that he understands her outburst, but he reminds her that he would have married her years before had she been willing. He has been her master once; he will be her master again. "If you are any man's wife you are mine!" He says he will leave her now because she has to return to work, but he will return for her answer to his offer later in the afternoon. He climbs down from the rick and Tess remains, silent and stunned. Then the machine starts operating again, and she goes back to her stupefying labor.

Comment

In the description of the threshing machine and its operator Hardy again indicates what seems to him the basically inhuman nature of the modern machine age. The thresher is a "despot," a "tyrant"; the engine is called the "primum mobile" (First Cause, God) of "this little world." The engineman is described as having the "appearance of a creature from Tophet," that is, from Hell. We are told that he "served fire and smoke," as opposed to the farm workers, who serve "vegetation, weather, frost, and sun." He never says any more than he must to the laborers, "as if some ancient doom compelled him to wander here against his will in the service of his Plutonic master." (Pluto was the ancient god of the underworld.) All these references point to the machine as being literally a hellish device and its operator a devil. Hardy's ideas on machinery and modern life have been indicated before, in the description of the train that takes the milk to London from

Talbothays (see Chapter Thirty), but there the train was not so much devilish as simply alien.

Now that Alec has changed his dress from that of a preacher to that of a dandy he more than ever resembles the villains of an old melodrama. "He twirled a gay walking-cane": all he needs to do to complete the picture is to twirl his mustache. It is in detail like this that Hardy's characterization is least believable to the modern reader.

After Tess strikes Alec with the glove, she is again compared to a bird in a trap, this time to a sparrow about to have its head twisted. Her words, "once victim, always victim - that's the law!" seem to sum up Hardy's attitude. She certainly is the victim being punished; we must ask ourselves why all this agony is being inflicted on her.

PHASE SIX: CHAPTER FORTY-EIGHT

In the afternoon Farmer Groby announces that the rick must be finished that day because the man and his engine are engaged at another farm on the following day. Thus the work goes on with even fewer interruptions than before. At about three o'clock Tess looks up and sees that Alec has returned. He waves and she understands that his temper has cooled down. The afternoon wears on and the corn pile gets lower and the straw grows higher. Even the strongest of the laborers begin to crumple with fatigue, and Tess's arms are working completely unconsciously, without any control from her numbed brain. She knows that Alec is still there, for there is an excuse for his presence now. Whenever a wheat rick is threshed, the gentlemen of the region bring over their terriers and their stout sticks, and they kill the rats that live at the bottom of the grain pile. When there is still

BRIGHT NOTES STUDY GUIDE

another hour to go before the ratting begins, Groby, much to Tess's surprise, comes up to her and tells her she can stop if she wishes to join her friend. The "friend" is Alec, and Tess shakes her head and continues working. Finally the base of the stack is reached and the hunting of the rats begins. The rats rush out of the rick in all directions and, amid the barking of the dogs, the screams of the women (Marian, half-drunk; yells that a rat has run under her skirt), the shouts of the men, and general confusion, they are pursued and killed. Then the last sheaf is fed into the machine, the noise stops, and Tess climbs down off the thresher. She is absolutely exhausted, and when Alec offers to walk with her back to her lodging, she accepts gratefully. He says that he still has some common human feeling and can feel pity and sympathy for her condition. He says that he has enough money to make not only Tess, but her whole family as well, very comfortable. Tess asks whether he has seen them and he says he has. He asserts that they do not know where she is, and that he found her by accident. Tess is ready to collapse, and the mention of her family is practically the last straw for her. She tells Alec to help them if he wants to, but not to tell her about it. Then she changes her mind - "No, no! I will take nothing from you, either for them or for me!" He leaves her at her door. She enters, washes, eats supper, and then immediately sits down and writes Angel a long letter. In it she begs him to come back to her "before something terrible happens." She is apologetic and admits that she cannot hope for his love. She admits also that the punishment he has given her has been deserved. But now, let him be kind to her. Let him come back so that she may die in his arms: "I would be well content to do that if so be you had forgiven me." She repeats again and again her utter dependence on him and need for him. She tells him that she is the same woman he fell in love with at the dairy, the same one who has loved him and been faithful to him throughout his absence. If he cannot come to her, then she begs to be permitted to come to him because she feels that something fearful may occur if they are not reunited soon. "Come to me - come to me, and save me from what threatens me! - Your faithful heartbroken Tess."

Comment

Hardy has several times drawn a comparison between Tess and a bird in a snare. In this chapter he employs the image of the trapped animal in a slightly different way, in that there is no comparison made between the position of the animals (in this case, rats) and that of a human being. Nevertheless, the **episode** of the ratting, in which small animals are run down and killed by "gentlemen", bears too much of a resemblance to Hardy's previous uses of trapped animals not to excite notice.

TEXTUAL ANALYSIS

CHAPTER 49-53

....

PHASE SIX: CHAPTER FORTY-NINE

Tess's letter arrives at Emminster. (Tess has been asked by Angel to send all letters to him through his parents because he keeps them informed of his address.) Mr. Clare reads the envelope and remarks to his wife that if Angel was planning to leave for England at the end of the next month as he had planned, Tess's letter would perhaps make him hasten his departure. Mrs. Clare, who ordinarily never permits herself to criticize her husband, says that he should have allowed Angel to go to the university like Felix and Cuthbert. Mr. Clare, like his son a man of principle, disagrees. He cannot see how it would have been right to sustain his faith by the same education to his irreligious son. Nevertheless, in his heart, he educating his two religious sons, and then to injure that faith by giving reproaches himself bitterly for the way the life of his youngest son has turned out. In fact, both of Angel's parents blame themselves for their son's unlucky marriage. They are not sure of what it was that caused

Angel and his wife to separate, but from words in Angel's recent letters to the effect that he is coming home to fetch her they gather that the separation is not permanent. Angel himself is at this moment riding a mule from the interior of Brazil to the coast. His experiences in South America have been unhappy ones. The fever he contracted early in his stay never really left him, and his illness, together with the difficult conditions and the disillusionment he has suffered, have weakened and aged him prematurely. Inevitably his ideas on life have changed. Having rejected the existing religious, he also began to examine and question the accepted ideas on morality. "Who was the moral woman? The beauty or ugliness of a character lay not only in its achievements, but in its aims and impulses; its true history lay, not among things done, but among things willed." Now that he has come to consider intentions as well as actions, he sees Tess in a different light. His judgment and behavior at that time now seem to him to have been hasty, and her image now comes to his mind accompanied by fond feelings. His change of heart was taking place at the time Tess came to Flintcomb, but before she felt herself free to write to him. At this time he was puzzled by her silence, and he misinterpreted it. He had forgotten the orders he had given, but she had not and was observing them exactly. He did not understand that her silence meant that she was bowing to his judgment, not questioning it in any way. Angel had a companion on the muleback journey that he was making. The man was an Englishman, a person who had traveled widely and had experienced much. And, in the way that total strangers will confess secrets to one another that they would never dream of telling to anyone they knew. Angel narrated to this man the circumstances of his marriage. Angel's companion, being sophisticated, saw these events in a much different light than did Angel. He "thought that what Tess had been was of no importance beside what she would be, and plainly told Clare he was wrong in coming away from her." The next day the man died. His death only magnified the force of his words in Angel's mind. By contrast, Angel now saw his own actions as petty and small-minded, and he was sorely ashamed of himself. From being her enemy, he now came to be Tess's staunchest defender. Such was Angel's attitude toward Tess as her loving letter was being forwarded to him by his father. (It must be remembered that, in those days of slow transportation, it would have taken many months for it to get to him.) Meanwhile Tess's hope that Angel would come rose and fell. While it was true that the facts that caused him to leave had not changed, yet she hoped against hope that he would return, perhaps in answer to her pleas, perhaps because he had experienced a change of heart. In any event, she tried to think of what she might do to please him in case he did return and she wished that she could remember the tunes he had played on his harp. Fortunately, she was able to inquire indirectly of Amby Seedling. Izz's lover from Talbothays, and Amby recalled several of Angel's favorite songs. Her spare time now was spent singing these melodies over and over. Tess is so wrapped up in her dream of a new life with Angel that she does not know that Lady Day (March 25) is here, and that Old Lady Day (April 6), the end of her engagement, is near at hand. One evening shortly before Old Lady Day, Tess is sitting in her room when someone knocks at the door and asks for her. It is a tall, thin girl whom she does not recognize until the girl calls out, "Tess!" Then she realizes that she is her sister, 'Liza-Lu. 'Liza-Lu tells her that their mother is seriously ill, and that their father is ill as well. Tess ponders the situation for a while and decides that she must go home immediately. While it was true that she was engaged until Old Lady Day, and that was only a few days off, she decides she must risk breaking her agreement with Farmer Groby. She wants to start at once, but 'Liza Lu is too tired to make the return trip that night. Tess determines to go anyway. She tells Izz and Marian where she is going and why, and asks them to make the best of her case to Groby. Then she gets 'Liza something to eat, sees her safely asleep in her own bed, and starts out for Marlott, directing Liza to follow her the next day.

Comment

The switch in the narrative from Tess to Angel is not the smoothest imaginable, but it is necessary because Hardy is preparing to bring Angel actively back into the story. Thus he must bring us up to date on what has been happening to him.

PHASE SIX: CHAPTER FIFTY

At about three o'clock in the morning Tess arrives at Marlott. There is a light on in the Durbeyfield house, and Tess enters. The neighbor who has been acting as nurse for Mrs. Durbeyfield tells Tess that her mother is resting but is still very ill. Tess takes her place at her mother's bedside. When daylight comes, she looks about and takes stock of the family's circumstances. The children seem not to have been cared for, and she resolves to minister to their needs. Her father is in poor health and, as usual, has few practical ideas for helping his family. His current plan is to send letters to all the antiquarians in England, informing them that he is the last of the d'Urbervilles and asking them to contribute to a fund to maintain him and his family as a kind of national monument. Tess, however, has no time for such fantastic schemes, for there is much that needs to be done. First of all, it is time for spring planting but neither their garden nor the plot of ground they have rented in the village has been touched. She persuades her father to care for the garden, while she and 'Liza-Lu see to the larger plot. Her mother's health begins to improve, and Tess is glad to be outdoors, no longer confined to the sickroom. She feels that if she can lose herself in the physical labor of planting she will not be disturbed by the worry and care that are perpetually in her mind. The Durbeyfield plot is one of about forty or fifty in a high, dry, enclosed area in the village, and it is there that Tess and her sister begin to prepare the earth for sowing. The weather is dry, and the farmers are taking advantage of it to burn up the dead weeds and other rubbish that have accumulated over the winter. Tess and 'Liza work through the day and continue past sunset. In the evening, illumination is supplied by the burning fires on the many plots. There is a strong wind blowing and it carries thick masses of smoke along the ground. The effect is to screen the workers from each other. As evening sets in, Tess sends 'Liza back home, but she, like many others, stays on to see that the planting is finished. She labors on, sometimes shrouded in smoke, sometimes illuminated by a flash of flame. She is so completely absorbed in turning the earth, all the while singing the songs Angel liked, that she is completely unaware of the man who labors beside her. He is dressed in an old smock; and since he is working the Durbeyfield plot, she assumes he is a man her father has hired to help her. Sometimes the smoke divides them; sometimes their digging brings them close together. She does not recognize him, but this failure causes no wonder in her because of her many long absences from Marlott in recent years. After a while he begins to dig close to her and, as she throws a heap of weeds on the fire, he does the same. The fire flares up, and she finds herself looking at Alec d'Urberville. The unexpectedness of his presence and the grotesqueness of his appearance (he is dressed in a very old-fashioned kind of smock) are frightening and comical at the same time. Alec laughs and says the scene resembles Paradise. "You are Eve, and I am the old Other One [Satan] come up to tempt you in the disguise of an inferior animal." Tess answers that she has never thought of him as Satan. In fact, she says, she has no thoughts of him at all, except when he does something that pains her. She is surprised that he has done all this labor only for her. He replies that he has indeed done it for her sake and also to protest against her working like this at all. Tess says that she liked doing it because it is for her father. Alec asks where she is going now that her engagement at Flintcomb is ended - "to join your dear husband?" She winces under the reminder and bursts out: "I have no husband!" He agrees, but he says that she certainly has a friend - himself - and that friend is determined that she will be comfortable even despite herself. She exclaims that she cannot bring herself to take anything from him. He says that he is thinking about her brothers and sisters. If Tess's mother does not recover, her father will certainly not be able to do much for his family, and therefore somebody will have to help them. Alec proposes that the "somebody" be himself. Tess refuses his offer protesting that her father, with her aid, will be able to maintain the family. Alec remarks that the entire discussion is silly because Mr. Durbeyfield is certain to accept help from Alec because he thinks that he is his relative. Tess says that she has told her father the truth about that. Alec, angry, now takes off his smock and leaves her. Tess is unable to continue working after his disturbing conversation and therefore begins to walk home. Just in front of her house she is met by one of her sisters who exclaims: "O Tessy-what do you think! 'Liza-Lu is a-crying, and there's a lot of folk in the house, and mother is a good deal better, but they think father is dead" 'Liza confirms the news: Jack Durbeyfield had died of a heart attack. His death is of more than personal significance because he had been a "lifeholder." (There were in the nineteenth century certain kinds of leases on houses and property called "lifeholds." They were called by this name because they extended over the lifetimes of three successive tenants and then ran out. Mr. Durbeyfield's was the third of the three lives on the lease of the family's house, and at this time it was the general practice not to renew lifeholds. This meant that the family no longer had a home and would have to move.)

Comment

When Alec appears out of the smoke and flame in the rented garden, he remarks that the whole scene resembles Paradise, the Garden of Eden, in which Eve was tempted by the devil. He quotes some lines from *Paradise Lost* by the seventeenth-century English poet John Milton, in which the temptation of Eve is described. It will be remembered that this is the second time a comparison to the events in the Garden of Eden has been made in Tess. In Chapter Nineteen, Hardy gives us another version of the seduction of Eve, but there of course it is Angel who plays his harp and attracts Tess. Talbothays is more garden-like than the landscape at Marlott, but the bareness of this garden and the smoke and fire are more appropriate to the devilish Alec, who runs everything he touches. Note that once again the scene takes place in twilight.

When Tess's father dies, Hardy remarks that the Durbeyfields had once been d'Urbervilles, and when they were rich and powerful had doubtless evicted many of their tenants just as they themselves were now being evicted. In this way the Durbeyfields were participating in the "rhythm of change," which "alternates and persists in everything under the sky."

PHASE SIX: CHAPTER FIFTY-ONE

It is now the day before Old Lady-Day (April 6) the day that the engagements entered into at the Candlemas Fair go into effect. The entire agricultural world is stirring because the annual migrations of laborers are about to begin. There is much more moving about now than in the days when Tess's mother was a child. Some of the changes are made simply for the sake of variety, but there are also larger forces at work. The farm population is growing smaller as more and more people go to the cities to try and better themselves. Previously there had been in the towns, along with the laborers, a different class, of which the Durbeyfields were a part. This was made up of craftsmen, like the carpenter, the shoemaker, and the smith, plus other workmen who were not farm laborers but held long-term leases on their houses. The distinguishing mark of this class is that its members did not move around from farm to farm. Their existence gave a permanence and stability to village life. But as the long-term holdings like the Durbeyfields' ran out, they were not renewed. Thus the way of life their residence in the villages made possible also came to an end. The eviction of the Durbeyfields is therefore, not only a great hardship to the family, but is also symbolic of the passing away of their whole world. Now that Old Lady-Day has come, the Durbeyfields must go elsewhere. On their last night in the place she had always called home, Joan Durbeyfield takes 'Liza-Lu and Abraham to say goodbye to various of her friends; Tess is left at home to care for the other children. It is raining and she is staring moodily out of the window. She thinks that she should never have come home because it is her presence that has ruined things for her family. When it was discovered by certain "people of scrupulous character" that Tess had returned and was living at home, Joan Durbeyfield was scolded for taking back her "no-good" daughter. An argument between these "respectable" people and Mrs. Durbeyfield took place, during which she offered to leave. She was taken at her word, and this was the result. Had Tess not returned, the family would probably have been allowed to remain as weekly tenants. She is so absorbed in her thoughts that she does not notice a horseman coming up to the house until he is practically at the door. He sees her at the window and makes a sign to her to open it. The rain having nearly stopped, she does so. It is Alec. He asks whether she did not see him and she says "no". She did, however, hear something, but it sounded to her like a carriage and horses. Alec says that she probably heard the ghostly d'Urberville Coach. She tells him that she was once told something of the legend concerning it, but doesn't really know the whole story. He tells her that it has to do with a murder committed long ago by a member of the family. This d'Urberville kidnapped a beautiful woman, who then tried to escape from the coach in which he was carrying her off. In the struggle "he killed her-or she killed him-I forget which. Such is one version of the tale ...." And since then, the story goes, the sound of the coach, which can only be heard by one of the d'Urberville line, occurs as a warning that misfortune will befall the one who hears it. Alec suddenly notices that everything is packed. She tells him they have to leave, and that she thinks it is her fault. She explains that "she is not a proper woman." Alec is furious at the small-mindedness of the townspeople. He asks where they are going and is told that their new residence will be in Kingsbere. Tess says that her mother has taken rooms there because the town was the home of the old d'Urbervilles, "father's people." Alec again offers the use of his house in Trantridge. Tess, unwilling, says that the rooms at Kingsbere have already been taken. And when the family gets there they can wait for ... Alec ends her sentence: "Wait-what for? For that nice husband, no doubt. Now, look here, Tess, I know what men are, and bearing in mind the grounds of your separation, I am quite positive he will never make it up with you." He again offers his house, and this time says that he will put it all in writing as a form of insurance for the family. Tess shakes her head, but Alec insists that she at least tell her mother so that Mrs. Durbeyfield may make up her own mind. He tells her that he owes her something because of the way he acted to her in the past, and also because she cured him of his religious "craze". She replies that she wishes he had remained in that craze because he would have continued to behave like a religious man. He asks her to give him her hand on the matter, and he puts his hand in through the window. "With stormy eyes" she pulls the bar that holds the window open, and in so doing catches his arm between the window and the wall. He is angered, but he says that he will expect the family, or at least Mrs. Durbeyfield and the children. Tess says she won't come because she has plenty of money at her father-in-law's. But Alec says that her pride will never permit her to ask for it. Tess remains at the window thinking about her situation. Suddenly she is overcome by the injustice of her position. Angel, like all the others, had been hard, very hard to her. She has never thought such a thing before, but she knows it is true. She also knows in her heart that never had she intended to do wrong. All her mistakes had been caused by ignorance, not by intention. Why, then, has she been punished so persistently? Bursting with these feelings, she picks up a piece of paper and hastily writes to Angel: "O why have you treated me so monstrously, Angel! I do not deserve it. I have thought it all over carefully, and I can never, never forgive you! You know that I did not intend to wrong you-why have you so wronged me? You are cruel, cruel indeed! will try to forget you. It is all injustice I have received at your hands! T." She sends the letter and then she reflects that it is hopeless. Why should he come? The facts have not changed. It grows darker, and Tess joins the four young children who are sitting before the fire. She tells them it is the last night they will spend there. They all grow silent, and it looks for a moment as if they are going to burst into tears. Tess changes the subject by asking them to sing to her. The four young voices begin a hymn they have learned in Sunday School: "Here we suffer grief and pain,/ Here we meet to part again;/ In Heaven we part no more." Tess listens and turns away from the fire in order to hide her tears from the children. If only she could believe what the words of the hymn so confidently asserted! Then she would gladly release her hold on life and leave them all in the care of Providence. But. as this is impossible for her to do, she must do something for them in this hard world: "To her and her like, birth itself was an ordeal ....." Soon Tess's mother, sister, and brother return. Joan notices the tracks of the horse and asks Tess who has been there. Tess says it was no one. The children "remind" Tess of the "gentleman a-horseback." Joan asks who it was-was it her husband? "No. He'l never, never come." If it was not her husband, then who was it? Tess tells her that she knows who it was; she has seen him before. Joan asks what he wanted, and Tess says that she will tell her every word he said once they get settled in Kingsbere on the next day.

Comment

The legend of the d'Urberville Coach is brought up again (Angel has spoken to her of it already: Chapter Thirty-three), and again the story is not told completely or clearly. It is significant that Alec doesn't remember whether the man or the woman is killed. Hardy is using the legend to increase our sense of fast-approaching doom and to foreshadow the death that awaits both Alec and Tess.

Tess's father had been convinced that he was the last of the d'Urbervilles; note that Joan Durbeyfield has also taken over this belief. The family is going to Kingsbere because it was the ancient home of "father's people." It is dramatically fitting that Tess's flight from Alec's desires should end at the family tombs, because the knowledge of their "noble birth" has brought them only misery.

After Tess tells her mother that it was not her husband that called, she is filled by a "consciousness that in a physical sense this man [Alec] alone was her husband." "A physical sense" refers not only to their sexual relations, but also to the fact that Alec plays the role of her husband in his desire to protect her, while Angel is nowhere to be seen.

PHASE SIX: CHAPTER FIFTY-TWO

Before dawn of the next morning the roads are crowded with wagons sent by farmers to the families of the laborers, along with their possessions, to their new homes. But for the Durbeyfields the situation is different. They are not laborers, but rather women who are neither needed nor awaited anywhere. Therefore they have had to hire a wagon at their own expense. When Tess looks out the window that morning, she is glad to find that the wagon is there and that it is not raining. Joan, Tess, 'Liza, and Abraham now go about loading the wagon. It takes several hours, but by two o'clock it is done, and the wagon starts out with all the Durbeyfields perched on top of the pile of their worldly goods. On the road they stop at an inn to rest the horses and buy some food. There Tess meets Izz and Marian, who have left Flintcomb and are going to a new place. They exchange their new addresses, and Marian tells Tess that Alec had come looking for her after she had left. Tess answers that he has found her and that he knows where she is going. Marian asks whether Tess's husband has come back and is told that he has not. Then the wagons start up again, going in different directions. The distance is almost too great for a day's journey, and so it is quite late when the Durbeyfields come to Greenhill, just before Kingsbere. At Greenhill, a man comes up to their wagon, learns that they are the Durbeyfields, and tells them that the rooms they had rented have already been taken by someone else. Joan's letter arrived only that morning, and by that time it was too late. Tess goes pale at this news, and Joan says, "What shall we do now, Tess? Here's a welcome to your ancestors' land!" They move on into the town, Tess remaining with the wagon while Joan and 'Liza look for a place to stay. When Joan returns an hour later to report she has not had any luck, the wagon driver tells them that the goods must be unloaded because he has to start back that night. The wagon had drawn up to a secluded spot under a churchyard wall. Joan says "unload it here," and the driver soon complies. She pays him (practically her last shilling), and he leaves. Tess looks around her desperately. They are near the site of the old d'Urbervill estate, and all the land she sees once belonged to her family. Close to them is the aisle of the church called the d'Urberville Aisle. Then Joan suddenly gets an inspiration: "Isn't your family vault your own freehold property? Why, of course, 'its, and that's where we will camp." In a few minutes the old large four-poster bed is set up under the d'Urberville Aisle, beneath which lie the tombs of the family. The smaller children are put in the bed, around which the curtains are drawn, and Mrs. Durbeyfield, 'Liza, and Abraham go off into the village to find some food. When they get to the street, they find a horseman looking up and down. He rides up to them; it is Alec. He asks where Tess is, and Joan (who doesn't particularly like him) merely points in the direction of the church. Meanwhile Tess has been talking to the younger children and making them comfortable. When they are settled, she walks around the churchyard. The door of the church is open, and she enters. There stand the ruined tombs of several centuries of the d'Urbervilles: the carvings are defaced and broken and the brass torn out. She approaches a dark stone on which is inscribed in Latin: "Then Gates of the Ancient Tombs of the d'Urberville Family." She cannot read the Latin, but she realizes that her ancestors lie buried here. The tombs impress upon her, more than anything else does, the fact that her family is socially extinct, and she muses upon this as she turns to leave the church. She passes an altar-tomb, the oldest tomb of all, upon which lies a figure. She would never have noticed it in the dark except that she gets an odd idea that the figure has just moved. She draws close to it and discovers it is a living person. She is so shocked and frightened that she falls to the floor, feeling faint.

As she drops, she recognizes that the man is Alec d'Urberville. He jumps up off the slab and supports her. He informs her that he had seen her come in and had lain down on the tomb so as not to disturb her. He stamps his foot on the floor, and a hollow echo is heard. "That shook them a bit … And you thought I was the mere stone reproduction of one of them. But no. The old order changeth. The little finger of the sham d'Urberville can do more for you than the whole dynasty of the real underneath … Now command me. What shall I do?" She tells him to go away. He replies that he will-to look for her mother. When he is gone, Tess sinks down on the door to the vault and moans: "Why am I on the wrong side of this door!"

Meanwhile Izz and Marian had gone on that day to their new employer. As they travel, they talk of Tess and Alec, whose connection with her past they have guessed, They understand that Alec poses a very real threat to Tess because he has won her once before. They know that they have no chance with Angel, and they do not want anything bad to befall Tess. They, therefore, decide that they ought to inform Angel of what is going on so that he might act as it becomes him to do. When they get to their new place, however, they become involved in establishing themselves there, and thus do nothing about communicating with Angel. After about a month they hear that Angel is coming home, and they decide to write to him. They write the following note and send it to him to his father's house in Emminster: "Honour'd Sir-Look to your Wife if you do love her as much as she do love you. For she is sore put to by an Enemy in the shape of a Friend. Sir, there is one near her who ought to be away. A woman should not be try'd beyond her Strength, and continual dropping will wear away a Stone-ay, more - a Diamond. From Two Well-Wishers."

Comment

Many modern readers find the incident in the church in which Alec jumps up at Tess from the top of a tomb to be overly melodramatic. It is important to keep in mind that this event is by no means unique in quality in the book, but that Alec and, to a large extent, Angel too (remember the sleepwalking scene), are drawn from highly melodramatic fiction.

PHASE SEVEN ('FULFILMENT'): CHAPTER FIFTY-THREE

It is evening at Emminster. Mr. and Mrs. Clare are expecting Angel at any moment, and they keep looking at the door and waiting. After a while there is a noise outside, and a carriage pulls up. Angel enters, to the heartfelt welcome of his parents. When he comes into the light, they are shocked to see him. He is thin and aged. He tells them that he has been ill, but that he is all right now. Immediately he asks whether any mail for him has come. He explains that it was purely by chance and only after much delay that he got the letter (from Tess) they had forwarded. Had he received it earlier he "might have come sooner." They ask him whether it was from his wife, and he confirms that it was. They hand him the second letter from Tess, which they have not forwarded because they knew he would have left before it arrived in Brazil. He reads the letter (see Chapter Fifty-one) in which she accuses him of having been cruel and unjust to her, and he says, "It is quite true! Perhaps she will never be reconciled to me!" His mother tells him not be so anxious about "a mere child of the soil." He replies that we are all children of the soil. He informs them now of her ancient and distinguished ancestry, and then he goes to bed. The next morning he does not feel well, and he remains in his room thinking about Tess.

While in his mind he had often pictured coming back to Tess and being greeted with open arms, in reality it was not going to be so easy. Her second letter shows that her feelings have changed, and he wonders whether it would be wise simply to walk in on her. He decides it would be better to prepare Tess and her family by sending a note to Marlott. In the says that he has come back and that he hopes Tess is still living there, as has been arranged when he left England. Before the week is out he receives a reply from Tess's mother which does not help him very much in learning the state of Tess's feelings. To his surprise it does not come from Marlott (there is no address of any kind on her letter). Mrs. D'Urbeyfield's letter says that her daughter is not there at present, and that she doesn't know when she will return but will inform Angel as soon as she does. She states further that she does not feel at liberty to tell Angel where Tess is. Angel takes the stiffness and formality of the letter to be a sign that the family is angry with him, but he is relieved that Tess seems to be all right. He feels that he deserves their anger, and decides to wait until Mrs. Durbeyfield informs him of Tess's return. A day or two passes during which he waits for a letter from her; he also manages to recover some strength. There is nothing further from Tess's mother. He takes out the first letter he received from Tess and reads it over. Her love for him, as expressed there, is so great and so genuine that he decides not to believe the tone of the more recent letter. He determines to go and find her immediately. He asks his father if Tess has ever applied to him for money, and is told that she has not. For the first time it occurs to him that her pride may have stood in her way and that she may have been in need. From his words his parents guess what were the real grounds for their separation, and their hearts go out to Tess. Angel packs a few things and is about to set out. As he does so, he comes upon the letter from Izz and Marian (see Chapter Fifty-two).

Comment

This phase of the book is entitled "Fulfilment" because in it each of the main characters fulfills his destiny. Angel, for instance, pays for his narrowmindedness by finding that he loves Tess just as he learns he must lose her. More important, he must bear the guilt of his part in Tess's death and also, of course, in Alec's. He becomes the man he should have been all along. Alec, who has led of life of violence, dies as he lived. He is punished, not so much for his first crime against Tess as for his treatment of her thereafter. His brutal persecution of Tess, although combined with a genuine desire to help her, is a major factor in her downfall. In large measure she has died at his hands; it is only right that he should die at hers. Tess's fulfillment is of several kinds: she avenges herself on Alec, she is at last reunited with Angel, and she meets the destiny (death) which "the President of the Immortals" had long ago decreed to be her fate.

Tess's luck is now always bad. Note that Angel says that he would have returned earlier had her letter reached him sooner, but of course it didn't.

TESS OF THE D'URBERVILLES

. . . .

PHASE SEVEN: CHAPTER FIFTY-FOUR

Fifteen minutes later, Angel leaves the house, goes to an inn, and rents a carriage. He drives to Flintcomb, where he assumes (because it is the address on the first letter he received). Tess is staying. He not only does not find her there, but also learns for the first time of the hardships that she suffered. He discovers that she never used the name for Mrs. Clare, an indication to him of how strictly Tess observed his demand for total separation. At Flintcomb she is told that Tess left without notice for her mother's house in Marlott. He knows that Tess's mother is not at Marlott, and he also remembers how unwilling Joan was to reveal her address to him. His only course is to go to Marlott and inquire there. Farmer Groby lends him a gig and a driver, and that night he stays at an inn near Marlott. He sends the gig back, and the next day enters Tess's birthplace on foot. Of course he finds that the Durbeyfields have gone, and that Mr. Durbeyfield is dead. The villagers tell him that Tess and her family were supposed to go to Kingsbere, but instead went to another place. He crosses the field in which he had first seen her at the dance (see Chapter Two), and all these reminders of Tess eat at his heart. He passes the local churchyard, where he sees the headstone which has been erected over the grave of John Durbeyfield, "rightly d'Urberville." The sexton of the church sees Angel bending over the grave and tells him that Mr. Durbeyfield wished to be buried at Kingshore, "where his ancestors be." However, his desire could not be fulfilled because the family did not have enough money. The sexton says that even the headstone has not been paid for Angel goes to the house of the stonecutter, finds it is true, and pays the bill.

He begins to walk, but after several hours finds that he must hire a gig if he is to make any time at all. He travels all day, and by seven o'clock that evening arrives at Joan's house. It was plain from the letter that she did not want him to come, and this impression is reinforced when he actually meets her. By way of explanation he says that she promised to write to him but had not done so. She explains that she has not because Tess has not returned. He asks where she is, and she stammers that she doesn't exactly know. She knows where she was …. He asks where that is, and Joan says that she no longer is there. It is obvious that she doesn't want to tell him Tess's whereabouts and he asks her whether she thinks that Tess would not wish him to find her. Joan answers that she is sure that is so. Finally he begs her: "Please tell me her address, Mrs. Durbeyfield, in kindness to a lonely wretched man!" Tess's mother sees how much he is suffering and at last says that Tess is at Sandbourne. She tells him that she knows no address, nothing more than that - Sandbourne. It is plain that Joan speaking the truth. He asks whether the family needs anything, and she replies that they do not. He then leaves, walks to the railroad station, and takes the next train for Sandbourne.

Comment

As Angel retraces Tess's path from Flintcomb to Sandbourne, the sad events connected with those places are recalled to the reader's mind. Angel has changed; he has seen the error of his former actions, and he now has our sympathy. At every step in his journey to find Tess he discovers some new evidence of her worthiness, and of the hardships she has undergone because of him. The chapter also develops suspense, because it is preparing the way for a dramatic meeting between Angel and Tess.

PHASE SEVEN: CHAPTER FIFTY-FIVE

Angel arrives in Sandbourne, registers at a hotel, telegraphs his address to his father, and then, at eleven o'clock at night, goes out into the streets of Sandbourne. It is a seaside resort town, set on the edge of Egdon Waste, a wild area that looks the same as it has since prehistoric times. Sandbourne is an expensive, exotic place, and Angel wonders how Tess could be living in it. There are two cows to milk and no agricultural work to be done. He guesses that she must be working as a servant in one of the large houses that he sees. Realizing that he can do nothing until the morning, he returns to his hotel. He sleeps hardly at all, and shortly after seven o'clock he is in the street, walking toward the main post office. He meets a postman and asks whether he knows the address of a Mrs. Clare. The postman shakes his head. Then Angel asks whether he knows of a Miss Durbeyfield. The postman replies in the negative again. At this moment another postman comes by, and Angel asks him about Miss Durbeyfield. He replies that he doesn't know anyone by the name, but there is a d'Urberville at an expensive hotel called The Herons. Angel gets direction and is soon there. It is very imposing, and he thinks that this is the last place he would have thought Tess would get work. He rings the bell and the landlady answers. He inquires for Teresa d'Urberville of Durbeyfield. The landlady asks if he means Mrs. d'Urberville. Angel says that he does, and he is pleased that Tess is passing as a married woman, even though she is not using his name. He asks the landlady to tell Mrs. d'Urberville that a relative named Angel has come to see her. He is shown into the dining room to wait. He reflects that in order to maintain herself here she must have sold the jewels that were given to her when they were married, and he does not blame her for a moment. He is somewhat nervous about how she will greet him, so changed does he look. He hears footsteps, and Tess appears at the door. She looks even more beautiful than ever, dressed in a cashmere dressing gown of gray and white. He holds his arms out to her but then drops them to his sides. She has not moved. "Tess! can you forgive me for going away? Can't you-come to me? How do you get to be-like this?" "It is too late," she says. He pleads with her that he was wrong but now he sees the truth. She keeps repeating "Too late, too late!" She asks him if he doesn't know her present situation-how did he find her? He says that he has made inquiries and simply found her. She stands and looks at him as if she is in a dream. Then she bursts out: "I waited and waited for you. But you did not come! And I wrote to you, and you did not come! He kept on saying you would never come any more, and that I was a foolish woman. He was very kind to me, and to mother, and to all of us after father's death." Angel still doesn't understand. She says, "He has won me back to him." Angel finally grasps what she has been trying to tell him; he sees her hands are delicate and that she no longer works. She says that he is upstairs, and that she hates him because he lied to her. She continues: "These clothes are what he's put upon me: I didn't care what he did wi' me! But-will you go away, Angel, please, and never come any more?" They stand looking at one another for a long, agonizing moment. Angel says: "Ah-it is my fault." He can say no more; it is clear to him that Tess has ceased to care what happens to her body. She is "allowing it to drift, like a corpse upon the current." Then Tess is gone, and he finds himself out on the street, walking aimlessly.

Comment

It will be remembered that Hardy made a point of contrasting the primeval, timeless quality of the woods outside Trantridge (where Tess is seduced in Chapter Eleven) with the cheap novelty of the d'Urberville estate. The same thing is done here when we are told that "within a mile from [Sandbourne's] outskirts every irregularity of the soil was prehistoric ... not a sod having been turned there since the days of the Caesars." This is the scene of the crime of passion that takes place in the next chapter. Always the new and the old are side by side, with the old witnessing events but making no comment on them. Notice also that when Alec can go nearly anywhere he wishes with Tess, he chooses to go to a flashy hotel in a seaside resort. It suits well with the flashy side of his character, the side that may be symbolized by his dandyish clothes, stylish walking stick and glossy good looks - in short, the side of Alec that derives from the hero of melodrama.

PHASE SEVEN: CHAPTER FIFTY-SIX

Mrs. Brooks, the landlady of The Herons, was not an overly curious person, but Angel's visit to her wealthy tenants the d'Urberville at such an unusual hour was enough to rouse her interest. Tess had spoken to Angel while standing in the doorway of the dining room, and Mrs. Brooks, within her own room nearby, could hear fragments of the conversation. When Tess goes back upstairs and Angel leaves, she follows Tess and stands at her door. The d'Urberville apartment contains two rooms - the drawing room (outside the door of which Mrs. Brooks was standing) and behind it the bedroom. She hears moaning: "O-O-O!: Then silence, then a sigh, and again: O-O-O!" Mrs. Brooks looks through the keyhole. She sees Tess upon the floor, her face bent over a chair. Then she hears Alec's voice asking what is the matter. Tess does not reply directly but instead starts speaking in a series of disconnected remarks: "And then my dear, dear husband came home to me ... and I did not believed you and gave way! ... and then he came back! ... now he is gone ... and I have lost him forever ... and he will not love me the littlest bit ever any more-only hate me! ... O yes, I have lost him now-again because of-you" She turns toward the door, and the landlady sees that her lips are bleeding because of the force with which she has clenched them. There are more words: "And he is dying ... and my sin will kill him and not kill me ... O, you have torn my life all to pieces ... made me be what I prayed you in pity not to make me be again! .... O God-I can't bear this-I cannot!" Alec makes a sharp answer to Tess's words. Then there is a noise-Tess springs to her feet. The landlady, thinking that someone is going to come out, hastily makes her way downstairs. She goes into her own room directly below, where she tries to listen but in vain. She then goes about her normal household activities, waiting for the d'Urbervilles to ring that she might go and clear away the breakfast dishes. She hears the floorboards creak as if someone is moving around, and then Tess comes down, fully dressed. She walks out, and nothing further is heard from upstairs. Tess does not return, nor does any sound come from the apartment. Mrs. Brooks thinks about what she has heard and what it might mean, and as she ponders the situation, she leans back in her chair. As she does so, her eyes stop at a spot in the middle of the ceiling that she has never noticed before. It grows as she watches, and she can see it is red. She stands upon a table and touches the spot, and it seems to her as if it might be blood. She goes upstairs but her nerve fails her - she cannot bring herself to open the door. She runs downstairs, opens the frontdoor, and goes out. She sees a workman she knows and she begs him to go upstairs with her. He agrees, and they both go back up and open the door. The breakfast is there, untouched. She asks the man to go into the back bedroom. He does so, and immediately calls out: "My good God, the gentleman in bed is dead! I think he has been hurt with a knife - a lot of blood has run down upon the floor!" The alarm is given, and soon the house is swarming with people. Alec's wound is seen to be small, but the point of the knife had gone right to the heart, and he lays there "pale, fixed, dead." Soon the news that a man has been stabbed is all over town.

PHASE SEVEN: CHAPTER FIFTY-SEVEN

Meanwhile Angel, dazed, goes back to his hotel. He eats breakfast, and then decides to check out. He takes his small bag, pays his bill, and leaves. As he is walking out, he is handed a telegram from his mother, stating that his parents are glad to know his whereabouts and that his brother Cuthbert is going to marry Mercy Chant. Angel crumples up the message and goes to the railroad station, where he finds there will not be any train leaving for more than an hour. He sits down to wait but finding he is too restless to remain he decides to walk to the next station and get the train there. He is some distance out of town when, pausing for breath, he looks back at Sandbourne. As he gazes down the road, he seems to see a moving spot. It is a human figure, running. Angel is still so numbed by what has happened that he only dimly realizes that it is someone who is trying to catch up with him. So far from his mind is the idea of Tess's following him that it is not until she is quite close that he understands that it is indeed his wife. She comes up to him, panting, and says that she saw him leave the station and has been following him ever since. He does not question her, but instead leads her off the main highway onto a footpath under some trees. When they are completely secluded, she turns to him and says: "Angel, do you know what I have been running after you for? To tell you that I have killed him!" He thinks she is delirious. She tells him that she has done it, although she doesn't see how she was able to do the deed. She has always had it in the back of her mind to do in return "for the trap he set for me in my simple youth, and his wrong to youth through me. He has come between us and ruined us, and now he can never do it anymore." She says that he never should have left her-she has always loved him so much. But she blames him no longer; all she is concerned about is that he now forgive her.

She is sure he must do this because she has killed Alec. "It came to me as a shining light that I should get you back that way." He assures her that he does love her with all his heart, but he still does not understand what she means when she says she has killed Alec. She answers that she has simply done it. Alec was taunting her about Angel, and it became too much for her to bear, so she killed him. Gradually Angel comes to understand that she is telling the truth, and his horror at the deed is mixed with his knowledge of the strength of her love for him. Apparently Tess does not feel the moral quality of her action; it is as if her moral sense has been extinguished completely. She is weeping with happiness on his shoulder. Angel wonders whether this crime of passion is somehow related to her d'Urberville blood. The legend of the d'Urberville Coach flashes through his mind. He concludes that her "mad grief" had temporarily unbalanced her mind and caused her to murder Alec. In any event, here she was, clinging to him "without a suspicion that he would be anything to her but a protector.... Tenderness was absolutely dominant in Clare at last." He kisses her over and over and tells her that he will not desert her, that he will protect her in every way he can, no matter what she may have done. They walk on under the trees. Every now and then Tess turns her head to look at him. Worn and aged as he is, she detects nothing wrong in his appearance. To her he is still her perfect, handsome Angel of Talbothays. "With an instinct for possibilities," Angel does not turn back to the highway but instead heads deeper into the woods. They walk, arms around each other's waist, together at last with no one between them, "ignoring that there was a corpse." They continue on for several miles, and then Tess asks whether they are going anywhere in particular. Angel replies that he doesn't know, but that if she can continue walking, they would go on until evening and then find lodgings in a lonely cottage. He asks whether she can walk, and she replies that she can walk forever with his arms around her. They therefore avoid main roads and continue in a generally northward direction. "But there was an unpracticed vagueness in their movements throughout the day; neither one of them seemed to consider any question of effectual escape, disguise, or long concealment. Their every idea was temporary ... like the plans of two children." At midday they come to a small inn where they can buy food. Tess wishes to enter but Angel tells her to remain hidden outside because her clothes are so stylish that they would be remembered. He soon emerges with enough food to last them for several days. They sit down on some branches and eat and then push on into the woods. Angel thinks that they should remain in the interior part of the country because he reasons that the police will be looking for them on the coast. "Later on, when they have forgotten us, we can make for some port." It is May, the weather is clear and warm, and it is pleasant walking. By evening they are deep in the New Forest. They spy a "for rent" sign in front of a large building somewhat off their path. Angel recognizes the building as a mansion called Bramshurst Court. He points out to Tess that it has obviously been unlived-in for a long time because the grass is growing over everything. Tess remarks that some of the windows are open; "all these rooms empty and we without a roof to our heads." He tells her that they will stop soon, and they continue onward. During that day they had passed several isolated inns and cottages, but their nerve had failed them and they turned away each time. As they continue to walk, Angel says that he has been thinking of staying at Bramshurst Court. They retrace their steps, and he tells her to wait for him while he goes to find the caretaker. He is away for some time, and when he comes back Tess is frantic with worry for him. He tells her that he has found a boy, who has told him that there is an old woman who serves as caretaker. She only comes to the mansion on fine days, to open the windows and air out the rooms. On those days, she comes back at sunset to shut them. They know they are safe, at least temporarily, and enter the deserted building. They explore until they come upon a bedroom, with a huge four-poster bed. At last they can rest. They wait until the caretaker comes and when she has gone they have another meal. Then they are "enveloped in the shades of night which they had no candle to disperse."

Comment

Note that it is May (spring) when Angel and Tess have their brief last period of happiness. Again, they experience their joy in the natural setting of the forest, after having fled the brightness and artificiality of Sandbourne.

PHASE SEVEN: CHAPTER FIFTY-EIGHT

During the night, which is "strangely solemn and still," she tells
him of his sleepwalking at Wellbridge. He asks her why she never
told him of it because it might have spared them all so much woe,
but she simply asks him not to think about the past. They must
live for the moment, for no one knows what the next day has
in store. The morning breaks wet and foggy, and Angel knows
that the caretaker will not be coming. He arises early and goes
to a little store a few miles off and buys food. His reentry wakes
Tess, and they eat breakfast. They are happy where they are and
have no reason or desire to move. In this way five days slip by.
They talk, but not of anything that has taken place since their
wedding day. Angel suggests finally that they might start toward
Southampton (a port) or London, but she is unwilling to move:
"Why should we put an end to all that's sweet and lovely!... All is
trouble outside there; inside here content." Angel peeps outside
and realizes that what Tess has said is true: "outside was the
inexorable." She confesses too that she is afraid that his feeling
for her might change, and were that to happen she would not
want to go on living. He assures her that he will always love her,
but she says she cannot see why anyone would not despise her.
She thinks of having killed Alec, and reflects that formerly she
"could never bear to hurt a fly or a worm, and the sight of a bird
in a cage used often to make me cry." They remain another day.
The next day dawns bright and clear, and the caretaker decides
to open the windows especially early that day. She silently walks
through the old mansion until she comes to a room in which she
thinks she hears breathing. She tries the door, but it has been
blocked by a piece of furniture so she can only see a small part
of the room. She sees Angel and Tess sound asleep, "Tess's lips
being parted like a half-opened flower near his cheek." Her first
feeling of indignation at these trespassers softens when she sees
their good clothes and innocent appearance, and she imagines

that they are an eloping couple. She closes the door softly and leaves to consult with her neighbors as to what she should do. Less than a minute after she goes, Tess and Angel awake. They both have an uneasy feeling that something had disturbed them, although they do not know what it is, and they decide to leave. It being good weather, they know that the woman will be coming, so they go immediately. They rearrange the furniture and depart into the forest. Tess looks back at the house and bids it farewell. She says that her life is only to go on for a few more weeks, and she asks why they could not have stayed. Angel tells her not to despair. They will push on to the north and get away while everyone is looking for them in the south. They continue as they have begun, avoiding settlements as much as possible. They are obliged to pass through Melchester at night because there is in that city a bridge over a river that stands in their way. They go through the sleeping city and, following the highway, enter onto a broad plain. The moon has gone down, and the wind is blowing. They have groped their way for a few miles when Angel becomes aware of some huge object directly before them, rising straight out of the grass. They have no idea what it is, and they approach slowly. Tess notices that it hums; that is, the wind blows through it and produces a strange "booming tune, like the note of some gigantic one-stringed harp." Angel runs his hands over the stone structure and finds that he is touching a huge rectangular pillar. By stretching out his arm he can feel another colossal stone column, and they can dimly make out a stone that joins the two pillars, making a huge "doorway." They pass underneath this arch and explore further, still without any knowledge of what the place might be. They find more of these columns and doorways, and also some huge stones lying flat on the grass. As they advance into the center of the group of stones, Angel suddenly understands that they are at Stonehenge. (Stonehenge is a group of huge upright stones, dating from prehistoric times, on the plain near Salisbury. It is in the form of two concentric rings of stones that enclose a central "altar stone," which was probably used in some ancient religious services as a place for offering sacrifices.) Tess is tired and asks whether they may not stay here for the night. Angel thinks they should move on because Stonehenge is visible for miles in the daylight. Tess recalls that one of her mother's family was a shepherd around here, "and you used to say at Talbothays that I was a heathen. So now I am at home." She lies down on a flat stone, and Angel, kissing her, remarks that she is probably lying on an ancient altar. She likes the place very much because it is solemn and lonely. She feels as if there were no one else in the world but the two of them, and she wishes that there indeed were none-except 'Liza-Lu. She asks Angel to assure her that he will look after 'Liza if anything happens to her, and he says he will. She is so simple and pure, Tess says. "O Angel-I wish you would marry her if you lose me, as you will do shortly." He replies that if he loses her he loses everything - and besides, she is his sister-in-law. Tess answers that marrying one's sister-in-law is common enough, and she wishes he would train her and teach her. "She has all the best of me without the bad of me; and if she were to become yours it would almost seem as if death had not divided us." She is quiet and thoughtful after these words. After some time, when the first signs of dawn are becoming visible, she asks Angel whether the ancient people of Stonehenge made sacrifices to God. Angel thinks they must have sacrificed to the sun. The mention of religion leads her to ask him if he thinks that they will meet as spirits after they die. He kisses her instead of answering and she knows this means that he thinks they will not. "And I wanted so to see you again-so much, so much! What-not even you and I, Angel, who love each other so well?" Angel cannot answer, and after a short time her breathing becomes more regular and she is asleep. The dawn begins to break over the plain, and the first sunlight illuminates the altar stone and the stones behind them. With the light Angel sees a figure on the horizon coming toward them. He wishes they had moved on, but thinks that the best thing to do now is to remain quiet. He hears a noise behind him, turns, and sees more men coming toward himself and the still-sleeping Tess. They are surrounded. Angel looks about for a weapon, but the nearest man says that it is no use. Angel begs them to let Tess finish her sleep, and when they see her they offer no objection. After a little while a ray of light wakens her. "What is it, Angel? Have they come for me?" He says yes, and she replies that she is almost glad. "This happiness could not have lasted. It was too much. I have had enough; and now I shall not live for you to despise me!" She gets up and approaches the men. "I am ready."

Comment

Some readers feel that Hardy's belief that the world is a cold and hostile place, a place in which such good persons as Tess are crushed, has been made clear enough without requiring Tess to be a "human sacrifice" at Stonehenge; other critics think the Stonehenge scene to be a daring stroke on Hardy's part and not at all excessive. By having Tess captured in Stonehenge, Hardy is saying that her destruction signifies more than the defeat of one individual. Stonehenge, as Angel says, is "older than the centuries; older than the d'Urbervilles." This means that Tess is doomed because the world, the physical universe, is basically the enemy of man and works to defeat his plans and hopes.

PHASE SEVEN: CHAPTER FIFTY-NINE

The scene is the "fine old" city of Wintoncester, on a July morning. On the western side of the city, there is a highway that ascends an incline which is a mile long. Up this road two persons are walking rapidly, hand in hand, seemingly unaware of the steepness of the hill. They are young, and they walk as if they are trying to get out of sight of the houses that flank the road. They march on with bowed heads, and the sun shines hotly upon them. One of them is Angel Clare and the other is a "tall, budding creature-half girl, half woman - a spiritualized image of Tess," 'Liza-Lu. When they are nearly at the top of the hill the clocks in the town strike eight. The noise of the bells makes them jump, and they walk the few more steps to the crest of the incline. They turn and wait "in paralyzed suspense." The whole city and the surrounding countryside are before them and against this panorama rises a large, ugly, red-brick building. Its front is covered with many barred windows and in its center is a squat, flat-topped tower. It is the prison, from which they have just come. Upon the top of the tower is a flagpole, and it is on this flagpole that their eyes are fixed. A few minutes after the hour has truck, "something moved slowly up the staff, and extended itself upon the breeze. It was a black flag." the sign that an execution has just taken place. Angel and 'Liza bow down toward the ground, as if in prayer, and remain in this attitude for a long while. "As soon as they had strength they arose, joined hands again, and went on."

Comment

The first sentence in the last paragraph in the book has given rise to much discussion: "'Justice was done, and the President of the Immortals, in Aeschylean phrase, had ended his sport with Tess." Obviously, what has taken place is anything but justice, and Hardy indicate so this by placing the word "justice" within quotation marks. Aeschylus was an ancient Greek playwright, and the President of the Immortals would be the father of the gods, or Zeus. Hardy does not necessarily mean Zeus, but rather the spirit of the natural universe, thought of as a person.

It has been widely felt that this last paragraph is a weakness in the book because it is unnecessary. The scene of the prison and the black flag is enough; Hardy's commentary, telling us what it is supposed to mean, is not needed. Equally, the final line, with its sight of Angel and 'Liza walking hand in hand into the sunset, is out of place. Hardy has, until now, striven so hard to make us feel the joylessness of man's existence that we cannot accept this last sudden hint of hope for the future.

It is interesting that many persons, including prominent lawyers and judges, wrote to Hardy at the time of the publication of Tess protesting that no court would have sentenced Tess to death.

TESS OF THE D'URBERVILLES

. . . .

TESS D'URBERVILLE

The heroine and main character of the story. Although she has more education than was usual for most girls of her class and time, she is still basically a simple country girl. (She regards Angel as impossibly far above her, intellectually speaking.) Although most of Hardy's country people are strong and enduring, Tess possesses these qualities to an astonishing degree. She is oppressed by misfortune after misfortune as the book proceeds, but not until the very end does she abandon hope and give way under the terrible strain she has undergone. Even then it is only because she despairs of seeing Angel, the man she loves more than life itself, that she breaks down. She consents to be Alec's mistress, but only because this seems to be the sole means of assuring the welfare of her family. When Angel returns, and the possibility of love reenters her life, she no longer can tolerate her position. She kills Alec, and runs away with Angel. Tess is the one morally sound person in a world otherwise populated by morally fragmented individuals. And it is this wholeness, along with her striking beauty, that is so attractive to Alec and Angel (and to the reader). It is, paradoxically, this very spiritual nobility that makes her so vulnerable to men like Alec and Angel, who do not and cannot commit themselves to another person as she does. she is the only major character (if we except Angel after he returns) who is not completely and disastrously bound up with his own ego. She is the only one who can care for others, who can enter into complete and satisfying relationships with others; she is the only one who does not exploit and use people.

It is striking how so many of the most interesting characters in fiction seem to be evil. The reason for this is that it is very difficult for a writer to make a pure, good character seem attractive to the reader. Such characters have a way of becoming too good, unbelievable in their saintliness. Hardy overcomes this obstacle; Tess comes alive at the start of the book and remains interesting and attractive to the end. One of the reasons for this is her resourcefulness. She is not trying to be saint, but is rather a person completely involved in the difficult task of surviving in an unfriendly world. Unlike so many "good" characters (and especially heroines) who are overly passive, Tess furnishes an example of goodness in action. When her life takes its downward turn, she does not crumble up and die but instead emphatically resists the misfortunes that assail her, and her very human determination and courage constitute some of her most appealing qualities.

ALEC STOKE-D'URBERVILLE

One of the two main male characters, the seducer of Tess, who kills him. He is rich, handsome, bold, dashing, sensual - the complete lady-killer. Although his last name is d'Urberville, that is not his true name; he is no real relation to Tess. Instead, he is the son of a rich merchant from the north of England who added the name of d'Urberville to his own name, Stoke, because it had historical associations and because the d'Urbervilles were supposed to be extinct. Thus Alec is a fraud as well as a morally corrupt person. Hardy takes pains to contrast his false nobility with the true moral superiority of Tess.

Alec is not a whole man, but only part of one. He is the personification of a certain kind of male sexuality. Until he meets Tess, all women for him are only sexual objects, to be exploited for the pleasure they can afford. Tess is different, and he is fascinated by her. He is fascinated because there is "something" about her that he cannot understand. This mystifying "something" is that Tess seeks love, while Alec does not know the difference between love and lust. And while it is true that his feeling for her deepens as the book proceeds, he is always inadequate for Tess because he cannot overcome this basic limitation. He is a prisoner of his own ego, basically too involved with himself to be able to give of himself to the extent required by love. Thus he cannot cope with a truly good and morally whole person like Tess, who has more to her than her sexual attractiveness. The other, higher dimension is a threat to Alec, a clear indication of his limitations, and he destroys her because he can do nothing else. A violent child of nature, he too has been corrupted by modern civilization. His tremendous passionate energy has no "natural" outlet. Thus he is driven to be a reckless sexual vagabond, and it is this same energy that makes him become a "fire and brimstone" evangelist.

ANGEL CLARE

The husband of Tess. Although in his personal characteristics he is the direct opposite of Alec, there are basic similarities between them that are more important that the surface differences. Both inhabit a moral and spiritual vacuum, both suffer from what Hardy calls "the ache of modernism" (see the Introduction for a fuller discussion of the moral climate of England at the time). One can understand their moral limitations best by comparing them to Tess, who is a whole, healthy person. In Tess, head and heart work together. In both the men, one aspect of their personalities has become overgrown and dominant, and therefore they are distorted beings. With Alec it is sexual energy that has gone unchecked, without any corresponding development of emotions to provide channels for it. Angel, on the other hand, is an example of a person who is governed by his intellect. He is more complex than Alec, and therefore it will not do to say merely that he is all brain and no emotion. More accurately, Angel's problem is that he has split his feelings from his intellect, and that his mind mistrusts his emotions. Because his emotions have developed, he can experience real, deep feeling, as in his love for Tess. Nevertheless, because of this separation between his mind and heart, he can make the cruel decision to leave her; his emotions do not take part in the decision-making process. He is capable of performing the most heartless actions, all the while saying that he is only acting rationally. In this regard he is much more cruel than Alec, who is frankly sensual and who does not pretend to any great emotional depth and fineness, as Angel does. Because of Angel's superior qualities, Tess does open to him; he seems capable of love. Then when she, who needs love more than life itself, has completely given herself over to him, he abruptly withdraws and crushes her. The injury he inflicts on her is therefore much more severe than anything Alec could have done. An interesting aspect of his personality is exposed at the time Tess tells him of her past. The shock is so great that all his intellectual refinement drops away, as it were, in a moment. The Angel who cannot see her except as a "fallen woman" is really judging her with the values, the ideas about "purity" that were implanted in him when he was a boy. In that instant he becomes again what he was before he came to Talbothays and learned something about the way life is really lived. It is significant that, bitterly disillusioned, he abuses Tess in the same snobbish terms that his brothers might have used: "Don't, Tess; don't argue.... You almost make me say you are an unapprehending peasant woman, who has never been initiated into the proportions of social things." This is a kind of moral callousness of which not even Alec might have been capable. (In Angel's behalf it must be said that he has within him the possibilities to learn, grow, and change; this Alec can never do.) One may suppose that Alec and Angel are two halves of one man. Each needs what the other has in excess. In any event, it is certainly true that Angel could have used some of his rival's direct, earthy sensuality to soften his overbearing and sterile intellectualism. When Tess first meets Angel at Talbothays, he is well described as "educated, reserved, subtle, sad, differing." Indeed, he is all of these and much more.

REVEREND JAMES CLARE

The father of Angel Clare; he lives at Emminster. He is "the last of the old-fashioned clergymen," absolutely rigid in his theology, which is of the most conservative Calvinist kind. It emphasizes man's fallen and sinful nature, the need for constant moral and spiritual self-examination, constant striving for a life of faith, and a perpetual search for the inner light that is the sign of God's grace. James Clare is very active in spreading his beliefs, and never hesitates to act upon them; he is an outspoken and very courageous man. His religious beliefs notwithstanding, in human terms he is a very good, almost saintly person. He is idealistic, unworldly, and attempts always to lead a truly Christian life. Because of this he is admired by his son Angel, who otherwise disagrees with him on matters of doctrine and faith.

MRS. CLARE

Angel's mother. She is religious, like her husband, but somewhat more worldly than he is. It is she who asks Angel whether Tess is "a Lady," while his father only asks whether she goes to church. She is less restrained than her husband, expressing her feelings more directly. She is a good woman.

FELIX CLARE

Angel's brother, a clergyman, curate in a church in a town near Emminster. Like his brother Cuthbert he is completely conventional. He is wrapped up in the petty cares of the genteel clergyman and has little imagination or sympathy for those who do not share his concerns and prejudices. He has nothing of his father's moral generosity or goodheartedness.

CUTHBERT CLARE

The other of Angel's two elder brothers. He is a clergyman, a classical scholar and fellow of Trinity College, Cambridge. Like his brother Felix he is completely involved in his own little world - in this case that of the university - and has neither interest nor understanding for anything else. Both he and Felix, though they have the education that Angel lacks, are completely deficient in humanity. They judge everything by appearances and are completely swayed by the opinion of the "world." They disapprove of Tess because of her "low" social station, which they think lowers them in the eyes of the world. They show the deadening effects of conventional education (remember that Hardy never went to college), particularly insofar as they have no spontaneous emotion of any kind. Moreover, though both are religious in a way that Angel is not, neither has any true religious feeling; in this respect Angel the nonbeliever resembles his father much more than they do. Cuthbert marries Mercy Chant, a fitting wife for him.

MERCY CHANT

She is the girl whom Angel's parents had hoped he would marry. Like the elder Clares she is extremely religious (her name implies as much), but in the quality of her religion and in her life in general she resembles more closely Felix and Cuthbert, Angel's brothers. Like them, she is completely conventional. She is concerned with the outward aspect of religion - details of worship and the like - but is completely lacking in the spirit of her faith. She is markedly deficient in the quality of mercy (and thus her name is ironic), particularly in the scene when Tess comes to Emminster for help. In her perfectly ladylike and respectable manner, she is a striking contrast to the passionate and emotional Tess. The difference between the two women marks the extent of the change that Angel has undergone.

JOHN DURBEYFIELD

Father of Tess and "last of the d'Urbervilles" is a poor, ignorant "higgler" (one who peddles from a horse and cart and otherwise does odd hauling jobs). He is a weak man, to a considerable extent under the influence of his wife, and is also largely a comic character. He would be quite enjoyable if not for the unfortunate effects his weakness and lack of guidance have on his family and especially on Tess. His health worsens as the action unfolds, and for the last part of the book he always seems to be celebrating his "noble birth" down at the local tavern. Like all the rest of Hardy's country people, he is fatalistic, accepting without protest whatever happens to him. He has a weak heart and dies late in the book.

JOAN DURBEYFIELD

Mother of Tess and wife of John Durbeyfield. She resembles her husband in her weakness, ignorance, and self-centeredness. In addition, she is vain and superstitious. However, Hardy makes it clear that she does possess a certain kind of folk knowledge and is rooted in a community and a way of life; and these are very valuable things. Moreover, she is basically a good person, foolish but always well-intentioned.

'LIZA-LU

The eldest of the six Durbeyfield children after Tess. She appears late in the story to fetch Tess back to Marlott. She is described as resembling Tess in her beauty, freshness, and unspoiled quality. Tess asks Angel to marry 'Liza-Lu after she (Tess) is dead, and she is with Angel at the close of the book. She is the only one of the other Durbeyfield children beside her brother Abraham (who appears very briefly) to have any significant part in the action.

IZZ HUETT

A milkmaid at Talbothays, a friend of Tess. Like all the other maids at the dairy she is in love with Angel, good natured, kind and ignorant. Also like the others she exhibits a strong amount of peasant fatalism. She is a loyal friend to Tess throughout. She joins Tess and Marian at Flintcomb-Ash.

MARIAN

Another of Tess's fellow milkmaids, and also in love with Angel. She is somewhat coarse and cowlike, and after Tess and Angel marry she begin to drink. She is working at Flintcomb-Ash and it is through her that Tess gets work there. She is a good, simple person and helps Tess whenever she can.

RETTY PRIDDLE

The third of the milkmaids at Talbothays, also in love with Angel. She is the youngest of the group, and she is very emotional. She inclines toward hysteria, and after the wedding of Tess and Angel tries to drown herself, but is rescued. Like Tess, her family (the Paridelles) was once great and powerful but has declined in the world.

FARMER GROBY

The owner of Flintcomb-Ash, where Tess finds work. He is mean, cold, and hard to all his employees, and especially to Tess, who he thinks has insulted him. He reflects the barrenness of his land.

MR. CRICK

He is the dairyman who manages Talbothays farm, where Tess and Angel fall in love. He is practical, unimaginative, and somewhat coarse; for all that, he is kind and well-meaning.

MRS. CRICK

She is the wife of Mr. Crick and is barely sketched in. We know little more than that she is something of a snob.

MRS. STOKE-D'URBERVILLE

Alec's mother. She is elderly and blind. She is a bird fancier, and hires Tess at the Stoke-d'Urberville house to care for the fowl that are her pets. She knows her son for what he is, disapproves of his behavior, but can do nothing about it. She dies late in the book, leaving the family estate to Alec.

CAR DARCH

A sensual, tempestuous woman, the one-time mistress of Alec. She has a quarrel with Tess which drives her into the arms of Alec and thus to her ruin. She and her sister turn up again at Flintcomb-Ash.

TESS OF THE D'URBERVILLES

. . . .

Because much of the story of *Tess of the d'Urbervilles* involves simple people who live in the southwestern part of England (which Hardy calls Wessex), who speak a dialect of their own, a list of dialect expressions and pronunciations and their translations into standard English is now given.

antiqueeruns: antiquarians

baint: ain't   ballyrag: bullyrag, abuse by scolding
barton: farmyard   black-pot: a sausage made of fat and blood   blooth: blossom

carking: anxious, distressing   clipsing: hugging
colling: embracing   cowcumber: cucumber
coz: cousin   crumby: plump, buxom
Cubit: Cupid   cwoffer: coffer, chest of drawers

dand: dandy   diment: diamond

fairlings: gifts   fancy man: a woman's lover
fend hands: guard, protect   fess: pert, lively

gaffer: fellow   gallied: flurried, alarmed   go azew: dry up
(said of cows)   green malt in floor: a girl becoming pregnant
before she is married

haggler: same as tranter (which see)   hagrode: hag-
ridden, beset by witches   higgler: same as tranter
(which see)   hontish: haughty   hwome: home

jints: joints

kex: dry stalk of various plants

lammicken: lambkin (term of endearment)   larry:
excitement   lift up a stave: sing a song

mampus: crowd of people   mead: (1) meadow, field; (2) a
fermented drink made of honey   mid: might
mistarshers: mustaches   mommet: spectacle

nitch: niche   nott: hornless (said of cows)

Oliver Grumble: Oliver Cromwell (English Puritan political leader,
17th century)

pattens: wooden shoes   pinner: pinafore   plim: swell
out   poppet: dear   projick: project   pummy: pulp

ramping: rampant, standing and reared up   randy: festivity,
party   rozum: a person with queer or fantastic ideas

skillentons: skeletons   strook: struck, rung
summat: something, somewhat   sumple: supple, smooth
swede: turnip

teave: struggle   tex: text   thirtover: perverse
tipple: drink   'tivity: nativity   tole: entice   tranter: one
who does odd jobs of hauling or peddling, usually with a horse
and cart   trowing: believing

vamping: walking about   vlee: carriage   volk: folk, people

whickered: giggled, snickered

zee: see   zeed: saw

There are in Tess, beside dialect words and pronunciations, other kinds of words and expressions that may give the reader trouble. These are foreign words, references to literary works, or words which refer to specifically English ideas or institutions.

Translations or explanations follow below.

Agape: a love feast, a meal eaten in common by early Christians

Aholah and Aholibah: prostitutes (in the book of Ezekiel in the Bible)

A mesure qu'on a plus d'esprit, on trouve qu'il y a plus d'hommes originaux. Les gens du commun ne trouvent pas de difference entre les hommes. "To the extent that one is more intelligent one finds that there are more original men. The average man does not find any differences between men." Pascal was a seventeenth century French philosopher and mathematician.

Antinomianism: The doctrine that, under the gospel, the moral law is of no use, and that salvation is to be achieved completely by faith

argent: silver (used to describe colors in crests, coats of arms, etc.)

Article Four: the fourth of the Thirty-Nine Articles that together constitute a profession of faith for believers in the Church of England

Ascham, Roger: sixteenth century English writer

Benedicite: prayer of blessing

bizarrerie: striking incongruity

Candlemas: February 2

Cerealia: feast of the ancient Roman goddess of growing vegetation

conning: studying

convenances: properties

copyholders: tenant farmers

corn: in England, grain and especially wheat

Cybele the many breasted: the great nature goddess of the peoples of the Middle East in ancient times; the mother of the Gods; the symbol of fertility

dapes inemptae: feasts consisting of food produced at home

Druidical: pertaining to the Druids, the priests and judges in ancient England

Evangelical: see Low Church

Friar Laurence: a character in Shakespeare's *Romeo and Juliet*

"God's not in His heaven; all's wrong with the world": an adaptation of the well-known line by Robert Browning: "God's in His heaven: all's right with the world"

guindee: stiff, unnatural

Hodge: name traditionally applied to the (nonexistent) "average" farmer in England

Huxley: Thomas Henry Huxley, nineteenth century Enlish scientist and philosopher, who coined the word "agnostic" (one who does not know whether there is a God, as opposed to an atheist, who denies God's existence) to describe his religious position.

ignes-fatui: will-o'-the wisps, misleading influences or things

"Integer vitae": first words in a poem by the ancient Roman poet Horace. They mean "the man of upright life"

Ixionian wheel: referring to the punishment of Ixion, in Greek mythology. He was bound to an ever-revolving wheel because he aspired to the love of Hera, the wife of Zeus

Lady Day: March 25

life-holders: a class of tenants who held their land during the lifetimes of three succeeding tenants. Upon the death of the third tenant, the land passed back to the owner to dispose of as he wished. Mr. Durbeyfield is the third life-holder on his property.

Low Church: the group in the Church of England (especially during the nineteenth century) that holds that the essence of the gospel consists of man's sinful condition, his need for salvation, and the necessity for spiritual renovation within the individual; it is synonymous with Evangelical and describes the position and beliefs of Reverend James Clare

Malthusian: pertaining to the ideas of Thomas Malthus, who said that the population tended to increase faster than the food supply, which meant that men must struggle to obtain food at the expense of others

National School: a school established by the Church of England in the nineteenth century to provide education for the poor

niaiseries: sillinesses, trifles

"Not in utter nakedness/ But trailing clouds of glory do we come": lines from the "Ode on Intimations of Immortality" by William Wordsworth

Old Lady Day: April 6

Old Style: the old days, specifically the times before the Gregorian calendar was introduced in England (1754)

Ostium sepulchrae antiquae d'Urberville: gates of the ancient tombs of the d'Urbervilles

parish relief: assistance given to the poor by the local government (parish)   partie carree: party of four (two men and two women)

Peter the Great: Emperor of Russia in the early eighteenth century

Pipe Rolls: ancient English rolls (documents) which were statements of the condition of the royal treasury. They date from the twelfth century

plantation: a grove of trees

primum mobile: first mover, God

Schopenhauer and Leopardi: nineteenth century pessimistic philosophers

springe: trap, snare

Stonehenge: a group of huge upright stones, dating from prehistoric times, near Salisbury, England. It is in the form of two concentric rings of stones that enclose a central "Altar Stone," probably used in some ancient religious service as a place for offering sacrifices. It is here that Tess is taken prisoner

Taylor, Jeremy: seventeenth century English religious writer   Thermidorean: referring to the month from July 19 to August 18 in the calendar instituted in France by the French Revolution

Uz, man of: Job in the Bible

Van Alsloot or Sallaert: seventeenth century Dutch painters of everyday scenes of town life

Weltlust: desire for worldly things

TESS OF THE D'URBERVILLES

. . . .

OVERVIEW

It is always true that our idea of an era (and its literature) changes as it becomes distant from us, because we are able to approach it without the emotional involvement natural to those who lived at that time. As the Victorian period (the later nineteenth century) has receded from us, it has become increasingly possible to attain such a (relatively) undistorted point of view. Thus the years since the Second World War have seen a great amount of critical writing devoted to a revaluation of Victorian literature. This fresh look, with its accompanying fresh judgments, has by no means come to an end, and criticism of Hardy has to be understood with this in mind. (Of course criticism is always a continuing process, and there are never any "final answers"; the point is that this condition is especially true of the later nineteenth century at the present time.) When we add to this interest in the Victorian period the fact that the twentieth century has developed several new critical methods and approaches for dealing with and understanding literature, it is natural that there should be a rather wide split between the older and the more modern critics. (The point of separation was probably the essays published as the Thomas Hardy Centennial Issue of *The Southern Review* in the summer of 1940, but this date must not be taken as absolute - there have been studies published after the war that embodied the older attitudes.)

THE TWO SCHOOLS OF THOUGHT

Basically, the difference between the two groups of critics lies in their idea of what the novel is. The older point of view, to be found in the books of Chew, Cecil, Duffin, Johnson, Rutland, and others (see Bibliography), is that the novel is basically realistic - that is, we value a novel to the extent that it imitates (in recognizable form) the life we see about us. Thus, for such critics, any overly pessimistic book cannot be very good because "life is not that way." Therefore Hardy, with his melodramatic action, grotesque humor, and frequent use of horror, presents them with a great problem. Hardy was and is extremely readable, and the general public has been attracted and held by his exciting plots and his deep feeling for the poor, for women, for animals, and for all those other persons who somehow have been dealt losing hands of life. Nevertheless, it is plain that Hardy's stories very often strain our ideas of credibility. In Tess, for instance, there has been much disapproval of the sleepwalking scene, of Tess's letter slipping under the rug, and of the fact that she is taken prisoner while lying on the sacrificial altar at Stonehenge. These highly improbable, even antirealistic event have been interpreted, by those who have not liked them, as examples of the bad influence on Hardy of a more old-fashioned way of writing novels that was popular earlier in the nineteenth century (specifically, of writers like Charles Dickens and Wilkie Collins). This interpretation may indeed be true; a character like Alec d'Urberville, for instance, does seem to owe much to the conventional mustache-twirling villain. Nevertheless, such departures from common life may be seen today in a different light. Since the serious fiction of the twentieth century has become increasingly sensational itself, Hardy's heightened action does not seem to a modern reader to be as extraordinary as it once perhaps was. Likewise, devices such as symbolic association (Tess amid the dead pheasants), coincidences, arrivals in the nick of time, and the like are more and more the standard materials of modern novels. Thus Hardy seems different to us than he did to readers who demanded fidelity to everyday reality (and not a special vision of that reality that might exist in an author's mind) above all. Finally, Hardy's awareness that the roots of love lie in sex and that marriage is often unhappy was unpalatable to a generation that was smothered in prudery and inhibitions that no longer pertain today. (The above discussion is drawn in large measure from Albert Guerard, *Thomas Hardy: The Novels and Stories*.)

MODERN CRITICISM

It is with this background that the following highly selective survey of the best modern criticism of Tess is offered. This does not mean that the older works are without value-quite the contrary. This arrangement has been adopted because it is felt that modern criticism will be more helpful because its attitudes are more likely to be more congenial to the student and because criticism is cumulative-newer writers respond to the work of the older ones and incorporate their work. The critics have been chosen because they have taken different approaches to Tess. They do not necessarily agree in their conclusions, but they do suggest several possible ways of looking at the novel, ways which are representative of present-day criticism, and as such they are valuable. The critics to be discussed are Harvey Webster, Arnold Kettle, and Dorothy Van Ghent (for complete references, see Bibliography).

WEBSTER

Professor Webster begins with a discussion of Hardy's intentions in writing Tess. Up to that time, a girl who was seduced in a Victorian novel nearly always embarked upon a career of prostitution or in some other way was completely ruined. But from the subtitle ("A Pure Woman Faithfully Presented") and the preface it is clear that Hardy is going to reverse this practice by making a seduced girl his heroine. This promises a vigorous attack on social standards, particularly those pertaining to sex. Now such an attack is basically optimistic, because the writer would not seek to change things if he did not think they could be changed; therefore, he is looking forward to a time when life will be different and better. Despite all this, it is striking that Tess expresses a pessimistic view of life in its emphasis on the all-powerful quality of fate. If men are in the hands of blind forces against whose power they can do nothing, then obviously the outlook is gloomy. We see such a view presented again and again in the novel: in the fatalism displayed by the peasants (the other milkmaids simply accept Tess's victory over them in the contest for Angel's love; Joan similarly accepts her daughter's seduction); in the way that Tess will not pray for Alec because she does not believe that any Supreme Power will change its plans because of her wishes; in the repeated comparison of Tess to a bird in a trap, completely helpless. The force that rules the universe is impersonal-it cannot be described more definitely than as "the rhythms of flux and reflux." "Flux and reflux" - Hardy seems to think that there are two of these vast anonymous forces. One tends toward pleasure, and the other toward pain; they are always in conflict. Such an opposition would seem to suggest that the lives of Hardy's characters are half happy and half miserable. But of course this is not so because, as Webster states, "the gods are persistent ironists." That is, when a character learns something through bitter experience, it is too late to put it into practice and make up the happiness that has been lost. A prime example of this is Angel's return after he has understood his mistake only to find that he is too late.

Professor Webster analyzes the ways in which these controlling forces operate in human life. First, there is heredity. Tess inherits her beauty and her precocious physical maturity from her mother, and it is this attractiveness that first brings her to the attention of Alec. In addition, she receives from her father's side of the family a certain lack of caution that also contributes to her trouble. A second law that regulates human action is that of sexual attraction. When a character is in the grip of this force, he is powerless to express his own individuality. When the four milkmaids are sighing with love for Angel, Hardy says that all four have become "part of one organism called sex." It is, of course, responsible for Tess's seduction and her consequent suffering and tragedy. The next great influence in the world of Tess is the great difficulty of earning enough to ensure physical survival. It is the poverty of the Durbeyfield family that brings Tess across the path of Alec in the first place, and it is Alec's ability to provide for the family that brings Tess to "sell" herself to him at the close of the book. Last, and by no means least, is the operation of chance. Chance always seems to operate against Tess-she happens to be fatigued and thus goes off with Alec when she would never have done so otherwise; her letter to Angel slides under the rug; when she finally goes to Emminster she meets Angel's unsympathetic brothers instead of his generous father. Yet, for all of this, Tess resists what is happening to her. She will not take the easy way out-she will not marry Alec when she can; she will not deceive Angel about her past.

Tess not only must contend with these great forces but, Hardy makes clear, she lives in a society whose rules have a great part in crushing her. When she leaves Alec to return home, Tess feels that she is a sinner because of the beliefs (which Hardy labels as delusions) that have been implanted in her by society. By the end of the book she comes to realize that she has been judged and condemned by a completely unreasonable and arbitrary moral law. Professor Webster asserts that it is possible to maintain that Tess's life would not have been tragic at all had it not been for the problems arising from social conventions. Had it not been for the disapproval of those around her, her seduction might simply have taught her something about the world without ruining her life. Angel, too, is caught in the bonds of convention. When he learns of Tess's past, he falls back on the attitudes he had absorbed when he was young, and is too blinded by them to see that Tess is indeed pure. Therefore, because society is so largely to blame for the fate that befalls Tess, one may argue that Tess is an optimistic novel, social arrangements can change and men in the future will not act as they did in the past. For Webster, then, *Tess of the d'Urbervilles* is a contribution to Hardy's "war against man's inhumanity to man."

KETTLE

Arnold Kettle takes a completely different point of view. For him the subject of Tess is not (as Hardy says) the tragedy of a "pure woman," but rather "the destruction of the English peasantry." Mr. Kettle sees it completely as a social novel - a novel with an idea at its core. This idea is that the "disintegration of the peasantry - a process that had its roots deep in the past - had reached its final and tragic stage." Everything seems to bear this out for Kettle - the death of the horse in Chapter Four is a "striking symbols of the struggles of the peasantry." In the opening chapters of the book there is "an immediate and insistent emphasis on historical processes." The discovery by John

Durbeyfield of his true identity is not merely comic but really announces the **theme** of the novel - "what the Durbeyfields have been and what they become." The ruin of Tess by Alec is symbolic of the ruin of the peasantry by the capitalists who have taken over farming. Kettle notes that after her seduction Tess sinks lower and lower on the social scale. She hopes to break out of her wage-slavery by marrying Angel but is cruelly frustrated. She goes to Flintcomb and there becomes a thoroughgoing member of the working class. "The scene of threshing is here particularly important, a symbol of the dehumanized relationships of the new capitalist farms." Kettle gives many more examples to support his idea that Tess is fundamentally a "moral fable," and not at all a realistic novel that narrates a personal tragedy. (Note that Mr. Kettle is here dealing with the same problem of nonrealism that the older critics dealt with, but he resolves it in a completely different way). He points out that there is much in Tess which rings false if we take the novel to be realistic, but which becomes understandable when we grasp that "its sphere is the more generalized movement of human destiny." Thus Mr. Kettle explains details like the unconvincing characterization of Alec, or the treatment of Christianity as all being part of Hardy's "moral fables." Kettle deals with the unrealistic tendency within Hardy's writing in a different way that did the older critics, who were forced either to disapprove of it or to accept it, and to justify their interest in Hardy by investigating his "philosophy." Mr. Kettle does not think much of Hardy as a serious philosopher, although he recognizes that Hardy certainly took his own ideas seriously enough. Rather, Kettle sees Hardy's conscious purpose, as expressed in the subtitle and the famous remark about "the President of the Immortals" (in the next-to-last paragraph of Tess) as irrelevant and misleading. For this writer "Tess survives Hardy's philosophy." It is Hardy's imaginative understanding of the destruction of the peasantry that redeems the book. Mr. Kettle says that Hardy's style, when he is making a "philosophical" statement, tends to be clumsy; but his style when he is describing and evoking the natural setting is magnificent. For Kettle, nature in Tess is not merely a backdrop against which the action takes place, but is rather an integral part of the book. The descriptions of nature make an important contribution to our understanding of the characters and the action.

VAN GHENT

If Mr. Webster has concentrated on the **themes** in *Tess of the d'Urbervilles* and if Mr. kettle has chosen to direct his attention to the book's social and historical aspect, Dorothy Van Ghent's excellent essay is most valuable, perhaps, in its discussion of the way the **theme** is expressed symbolically. Like Mr. Kettle she does not have much respect for Hardy when he attempts philosophical statements, and consequently, she discounts the worth of any estimate of Hardy which is based on his philosophy. For her, such statements "break into" the novel and are irrelevant. For example, concerning that sentence once again that speaks of the "President of the Immortals," she thinks it does not belong there because it intrudes - the sight of the gallows would be enough to convey Hardy's meaning. His "vision (of Tess's death) is deep and clear enough" without his interpreting the event for the reader and telling him what to think about it. For Mrs. Van Ghent, the important thing about an author's philosophy in a novel is how it gets translated into meaningful imaginative expression, not how many isolated "ideas" of the author the reader can pick out. Her essay is largely an attempt to point out just how Hardy does this - that is, how he express imaginatively his vision and understanding of the world. (Many of her comments have been included in the detailed summary of Tess which precedes.) She agrees with Mr. Kettle that Hardy's masterful presentation of nature is one of the truly excellent aspects of the novel. Both critics feel that (in Mrs. Van Ghent's words) "the earth is most actual as a dramatic factor - that is, as a factor of causation; and by this we refer simply to the long stretches of earth that have to be trudged in order that a person may get from one place to another, the slowness of the business, the irreducible reality of it ... its grimness of soul-wearying fatigue...." She points out how appearances have an added symbolic dimension in Tess - that is, Hardy's descriptions seem to gain a kind of depth because they direct our attention to some larger meaning. An example: Blackmoor Vale is presented in such a way that we see it clearly, but the words used by Hardy also suggest "the vale of birth, the cradle of innocence." Talbothays dairy, described in all its lushness, is for Mrs. Van Ghent a rendering of the "sensual dream, the lost Paradise." The discussion of the dramatic importance of the earth and the lost Paradise brings us to Mrs. Van Ghent's basic understanding of Tess. She thinks that the book's "subject is mythological, for it places the human **protagonist** [Tess] in dramatic relationship with the nonhuman and orients his destiny among preternatural powers." This "nonhuman" element, the earth, is basically hostile to Tess, who struggles to assert her consciousness against this unyielding opponent. What makes Tess's situation tragic is that she, too, is not pure consciousness but is "earth" as well - that is, she is flesh and blood and thus is contending against herself when she contends with "earth." The preoccupation of this critic with mythic elements naturally causes her to examine other nonrational things in the story, such as the fatalistic acceptance that the peasants display and their completely natural belief in magic. Her approach also determines her interpretation of the characters-to her they are fundamentally supernatural, as befits a drama in which the participants are larger than human. Angel's name is no accident, nor is the fact that he plays a harp (see comment on Chapter Nineteen in the detailed summary). Similarly, she accepts the resemblances between Alec and the devil (particularly noticeable in Chapter Fifty, in which Alec emerges smiling, pitchfork in hand, from the smoke and flame around the planting fires) as perfectly appropriate to the scheme of the book. She even thinks that Alec is so named because he is "the smart aleck of the Book of Job," that is, the devil. That Alec is converted to religion is also in character "because he is not really so very different from Angel (the smart aleck of the Book of Job was also an angel), for extreme implies extreme, and both Angel and Alec are foundered in egoism, the one in idealistic egoism, the other in sensual egoism, and Angel himself is diabolic enough in his prudery."

Tess of the d'Urbervilles has given rise to a great deal of criticism, and the student should bear in mind that the summary he has just read does not contain the "last word" on the novel. It is not claimed that everything these writers have said is correct, nor is it necessary for the student to agree with all of it. The use of such a summary lies in its suggestion to the student of possibilities, of ways of seeing and thinking about the book. It should be borne in mind that the main thing a critic brings to a book is not a great deal of specialized knowledge but rather a willingness to read as closely, carefully, and sensitively as he can, and then to think hard about what he has read and what it might mean. If the student is ready to do as much, then his experience of the book will have great value.

TESS OF THE D'URBERVILLES

Question: What is Hardy's attitude toward religion, as revealed in Tess?

Answer: It is perhaps tempting to say that since Hardy himself was an atheist, the portrayal of religion in Tess will be negative. However, a novelist never simply puts his own ideas straight into the mouths of his characters, but he seeks to create lifelike persons, each with a mind and heart of his own. Therefore, the answer to a question like this cannot be found in Hardy's biography (although his experiences are undoubtedly important), but in a close examination of the way the characters in the novel speak and act. Before we do that we must remind ourselves that Tess is a novel that probes deeply into the questions that were agitating England at that time, and that perhaps foremost of these (for young people especially) was determining the proper role of religion in life. In 1859 Charles Darwin had published *The Origin of Species*, in which he announced that all life that we see around us today has evolved from other, lower forms of life over millions and millions of years. This concept of development by evolution did not agree with the account of the creation of life given in the Bible, and thinking people immediately began to feel the difficulties of living a world without God. Many felt that if the Bible was the word of God, and if it now was in conflict with what science showed to be true, then belief in the Bible and in God became impossible. Ever since that time England (and the world) has been struggling with the conflict between science and religion, and *Tess of the d'Urbervilles* can be seen as Hardy's attempt to examine the effects of living in the world after Darwin. Remember that Tess was born in 1867 - that is, she is in the first post-Darwinian generation.

A good way of approaching our question is to begin with Reverend James Clare. He is a truly good man, wholly dedicated and sincere in his beliefs, and respected even by Angel, who is an unbeliever. He is the only religious person in the book who was Hardy's respect and admiration. But even this admiration must be qualified by the depiction of the good clergyman's activities. Let us start at home: of his sons, who have had the example of his pious behavior all their lives, one is an unbeliever and the other two are wordly hypocrites. We see two of his converts: the man with the red paint who walks through the countryside daubing Biblical texts on walls - an ignorant fanatic - and then there is Alec. Clearly Reverend James Clare has not been as successful in spreading the word of God as he might have been. An explanation for this failure may perhaps be found in his theology. His Christianity is one that emphasizes man's sinful nature. In it man is pictured as a creature who is always ready and willing to sin and who therefore requires a great deal of correction in order to be saved. This correction is not easy to achieve because man's erring impulses are very strong. Therefore, a Christian, according to these ideas, should inspect all his natural impulses and repress most of them. Hardy has a brilliant insight when he suggests that Alec's religious fervor and his animal sensuality are two sides of the same coin, the coin of his passionate energy. Anything Alec does he does wholeheartedly. The force with which he represses his sexual impulses after he is converted is the same force with which he expressed those impulses in pursuing Tess. Hardy's understanding of this makes Alec's conversion and his subsequent return to his old ways completely convincing.

Angel, whom Hardy calls a representative young man of the times, offers another side of the religious problem at the end of the last century. He is a person who has been directly affected by the conflict between science and religion. Although he admires his father as a man, he is at bottom a rationalist-he must have reasons for his beliefs. He is able to think his way out of religion but lacks the strength of mind necessary to construct some substitute for it. Thus he is left high and dry; he behaves as if he were a Christian, but he does not accept the religion that would serve as a firm base and justification for his conduct. This profound moral confusion lies at the root of his heartlessness toward Tess. For Angel acts in what is really a much worse way toward her than does Alec. Alec seduces her, it is true, but he is the first to acknowledge that he has been unable to touch her soul. Angel, however, violates her spiritually and in the most unpleasant way. Moreover, Angel's religious doubts are no abstract set of intellectual statements, without connection to the rest of the events of the story. On the contrary, it was precisely the crisis in his period of religious doubts that brought about his "eight and forty hours of dissipation with a stranger," and it is his admission of this that brings about Tess's confession about her past with Alec.

As to Tess herself, she too loses faith in the religious teachings of her youth, but because of her innate moral strength suffers least from it. As a child she instinctively showed true religious compassion for suffering animals and in her natural tenderness toward her brothers and sisters. It is her experience with Alec, which is capped by the brutal insensitivity of the "religious" man with the red paint, that convinces her that her childish ideas of God are inadequate. As she learns more about the evil of the world this feeling grows within her. Thus, when she meets Angel she need not be able to understand his arguments against religion to be brought to agree with him: she has come to much the same nonreligious position by herself without having the words to phrase it.

In conclusion, therefore, one might say that Hardy has little good to say for religion. The only persons who earn his respect are those who behave as good persons, no matter what they happen to believe or not to believe. Basically, Hardy's main objection to religion is that it does offer an adequate explanation for the facts of existence. In terms of human behavior, religion for most persons has a bad effect because it tends to screen out unpleasant aspects of reality. Because people feel that religion has given them the answers to certain questions, it is no longer necessary for them to think about these things. Therefore it provides them with a set of ready-made attitudes and, like any prejudice, acts to prevent people from confronting life squarely. And, at worst, it can be a respectable cloak that can be used to hide all sorts of moral deception and blindness.

Question: Discuss Hardy as a modern writer.

Answer: Thomas Hardy wrote at a time when the novel was undergoing great changes as a literary form. For it was at the end of the nineteenth century that the attitudes, devices, and **themes** that are typical of modern serious fiction were being developed. In order to be able to come to some judgment of Hardy's place in literary history we must first be clear about the characteristics of the modern novel, especially as concerns **theme**, style, and the relation of the novelist to his work and to society.

The characteristic **theme** of the modern novel is the isolation of man in a hostile or morally indifferent world; the approach is pre-eminently psychological, with great attention paid to an examination of inner motivations and complicated states of mind; the style is usually complex and often difficult, with much concern for complicated structural devices and for the point of view from which the story is told; and the novelist thinks of himself as not merely telling an amusing or interesting story but as creating a whole fictional world which will be the embodiment of his understanding and vision of life-he is a man whose work must be judged by artistic standards, and he does not expect to be understood by more than the small public who can properly apply such standards. If we accept these statements as generally true, then it is clear that Hardy cannot correctly be classified as a modern writer. Hardy always regarded himself as primarily a storyteller, and many critics have stressed his connection with the taletellers of olden days, who were the popular entertainers in an age when means of mass entertainment did not exist. In addition, he consciously strived for popularity, and was very sensitive to the requirements and standards of the reading public. He never took special pains over the writing of his novels. When his style is difficult it is usually because the writing is graceless or clumsy and not because he is self-consciously attempting to create a complex verbal structure. He is not at all a psychological writer, as we understand that term today; his novels are not filled with detailed and painstaking analyses of his characters' souls, as are the works of his contemporaries Henry James or Joseph Conrad. Nor was Hardy an especially sophisticated man, with a very subtle mind. It is true that Tess can be seen as an examination of several problems or tendencies within English society, among which is the effects of spiritual isolation. In this, Hardy is undoubtedly modern, but this is not the main source of his strength. We read Hardy today for the power with which he creates a world now lost, and for the tragic vision of life which he presents so well. Thus, while Hardy has some characteristics of the modern writer, it is probably more accurate to view him as the last of the Victorians, the last of the great nineteenth century writers who were responsible for the flowering of the modern English novel.

Question: Discuss the central images of *Tess of the d'Urbervilles*.

Answer: It is tempting, when discussing a novel, to concentrate on the **theme** - that is, to try to make some statement which will sum up the meaning of the book. While there is nothing wrong with doing this, it tends to be dangerous because the reader gets to thinking that this is either the best or indeed the only way of talking about a novel. But some thought makes it plain that what distinguishes a novel from other kinds of prose is precisely its overall narrative aspect (a group of essays can have a **theme**, too). Only within the framework of the unfolding of the story does the detail-incident, figurative language, etc. - have any meaning. The critic John Holloway has said that this overall movement in Tess may be grasped in the form of several metaphors. The first is the hunting of an animal. We remember the frequent comparisons of Tess to a bird in a snare: the night she spends in the field with the dying pheasants, with whom she explicitly identifies herself; and of course the fact that she is captured on the altar at Stonehenge, where the ancient inhabitants of England used to offer up animal sacrifices to the gods. **Metaphor**, then, is a way of communicating meaning through other means than direct statement. Holloway finds this **metaphor** of the hunt to be part of a larger metaphor - that of Tess as representative of the human race, and the course of her life being a miniature version of the establishment, decline, and death of the human species. Holloway thus sees Hardy fashioning **metaphors** from Darwinian evolutionary biology to convey his profound pessimism about human life.

Question: Discuss Hardy's view of the relationship between man and nature as it appears in Tess.

Answer: Although the following statement was made in 1917, a quarter of a century after the publication of Tess, it will serve well to present Hardy's view of the relation between man and the natural world. He was speaking about a book of his poems that had just come out: "I do not expect much notice will be taken of these poems; they mortify the human sense of self-importance by showing, or suggesting, that human beings are of no matter or appreciable value in this nonchalant universe." Because man cannot understand the vast order of nature, it appears indifferent to him, his aims and desires-it is "nonchalant." Nature cannot be controlled or interfered with; it proceeds at its own pace. Those who realize this simply accept everything as it comes. Those who do not may try to resist the impulses of nature but will inevitably be unsuccessful in their efforts. The peasants in Tess provide the best example of the first course of action. They simply accept life. For example, the other milkmaids do not complain when Tess wins Angel's love; similarly, Tess's parents accept what has happened to her when she returns from Trantridge-as Joan Durbeyfield says; "Well, we must make the best of it, I suppose. 'Tis nater, after all, and what do please God!"

However, what happens when man takes the second course and resists the working of nature? Then we have tragedy. Here another statement by Hardy is appropriate: "The best tragedy-highest tragedy in short-is that of the worthy encompassed by the inevitable. The tragedies of immoral and worthless people are not of the best." The "best tragedy" of course is exactly what happens in Tess. In the world of the novel, Tess is clearly the finest person, the most complex, the one with the most potential-in short, the most worthy. It is Hardy's great accomplishment that we feel that she is overcome by an inevitable force, that is, by the order of nature (here nature includes human as well as nonhuman events because nature is the cause of all of them).

It must be said that many readers have not found Hardy's universe to be strictly neutral, however inescapable it may be. It often seems that nature actively opposes human plans, particularly those of the best humans (i.e., Tess). When Tess is seduced by Alec, Hardy meditatively says "... why [it is that] so often the coarse appropriates the finer thus, the wrong man the woman, the wrong woman the man, many thousand years of analytical philosophy have failed to explain to our sense of order." This statement and others like it seem to imply that Hardy feels that there is a pattern that prevails in the universe, and that the pattern is a hostile one. Disasters such as those that befall Tess, Hardy seems to be saying, occur on purpose, insofar as we can detect a purpose.

Of course the worthy are not encompassed by the inevitable acting only through the order of physical nature. The tragic hero is trapped between the onward march of nature and the stupidity of human laws and arrangements. Often enough, natural law is to be preferred to the manmade variety. Thus, when Tess returns pregnant from Trantridge, Hardy comments that her misery is needlessly self-imposed because "she had been made to break an accepted social law, but no law known to the environment in which she fancied herself such an anomaly."

BIBLIOGRAPHY AND GUIDE TO RESEARCH

. . . .

TEXT

Hardy published many of his novels, including *Tess of the d'Urbervilles*, in magazines before they were brought out in book form. This is because magazine editors often demanded that Hardy rewrite large sections of his books that were thought to be too outspoken and frank. This Hardy did, but then proceeded to restore the text to the original form when it appeared as a book. However, at this time the works of foreign authors were not protected by copyright laws in the United States, and thus many of Hardy's works were printed, without his permission, in book form in the United States using the bad text that had been published in the magazines. Unfortunately, many of these editions using the bad text are still available, and you should be careful to avoid them. Any edition of Hardy's works that has appeared recently (including any of the paperbacks now in print) is sure to be based on the good text. This "good text," the standard edition of Hardy's works, is called the Wessex edition and appeared in twenty-two volumes from 1912 to 1922. Hardy was also a notable poet, and his *Collected Poems* is published by Macmillan in New York.

BIOGRAPHY

The standard biography is that compiled by Hardy's second wife, Florence Emily Hardy - "compiled" rather than "written," because much of the work of writing as well as that of assembling the letters, diaries, notebooks, etc., was done by Hardy himself. It is in two volumes: *The Early Life of Thomas Hardy*, 1840–1891 (1928) and *The Later Years of Thomas Hardy*, 1892–1928 (1930). These two have been reissued in a single volume as *The Life of Thomas Hardy* (1962). There are two readable shorter biographical works: *Evelyn Hardy, Thomas Hardy: A Critical Biography* (1954), and Carl Weber, *Hardy of Wessex: His Life and Literary Career* (1962). Chapter twelve of Weber's book is good on persons and events concerned with the publication of *Tess of the d'Urbervilles*.

CRITICAL WORKS GENERAL:

Abercrombie, Lascelles. *Thomas Hardy: A Critical Study* (1912).

Bailey, J. O. *Thomas Hardy and the Cosmic Mind* (1956). Best book on Hardy's ideas.

Beach, Joseph Warren. *The Technique of Thomas Hardy* (1922).

Blunden, Edmund. *Thomas Hardy* (1942).

Brown, Douglas. *Thomas Hardy*. (1954). Recommended.

Chew, Samuel. *Thomas Hardy: Poet and Novelist* (1928).

Cecil, Lord David. *Hardy the Novelist* (1943).

Guerard, Albert. *Thomas Hardy: The Novels and Stories* (1949). Probably the best overall book on Hardy, although not especially valuable for *Tess*.

Holloway, John. *The Charted Mirror* (1960).

Holloway, John. *The Victorian Sage* (1953).

Johnson, Lionel. *The Art of Thomas Hardy* (1894). The first book on Hardy.

Lawrence, D. H. "A Study of Thomas Hardy," in *Phoenix* (reprinted 1961), pp. 398–516.

Rutland, William. *Thomas Hardy: A Study of the Writings and Their Background* (1938).

Webster, Harvey. *On a Darkling Plain* (1947). Recommended.

Wing, George. *Thomas Hardy* (1963). (Evergreen paperback.) Excellent short survey.

Perhaps the most important collection of essays on Hardy appeared in the Thomas Hardy Centennial number of *The Southern Review*, VI (Summer 1940). These essays mainly consider Hardy as a poet, although there are several on his novels. An excellent collection of essays on Hardy was edited by Albert Guerard in the *Twentieth Century Views Series*, published in paperback by Prentice-Hall (1963). It reprints, among other things, four of the articles from *the Southern Review* issue on Hardy (which is hard to find), along with the Van Ghent essay on Tess (see below) and much more.

ON TESS OF THE D'URBERVILLES:

There are chapters or sections on *Tess* in many of the above titles; in addition, the following are recommended:

Kettle, Arnold. *"Tess of the d'Urbervilles,"* in *An Introduction to the English Novel* (Harper Torchbook paperback, 1960), II, 49–62.

Van Ghent, Dorothy. "On *Tess of the d'Urbervilles,"* in *The English Novel: Form and Function* (Harper Torchbook paperback, 1961), pp. 195–209.

The respective introductions to the *Modern Library* (1951) and *Riverside* (1960 paperback editions of Tess by Carl Weber and William Buckler are valuable. Professor Weber includes a useful map of Hardy's Wessex, while Professor Buckler offers more perceptive critical comments.

Perhaps the most important thing the student can do in preparing a paper on Hardy is to read other of his novels. Recommended are *Return of the Native, The Mayor of Casterbridge,* and *Jude the Obscure,* all readily available in paperback editions.

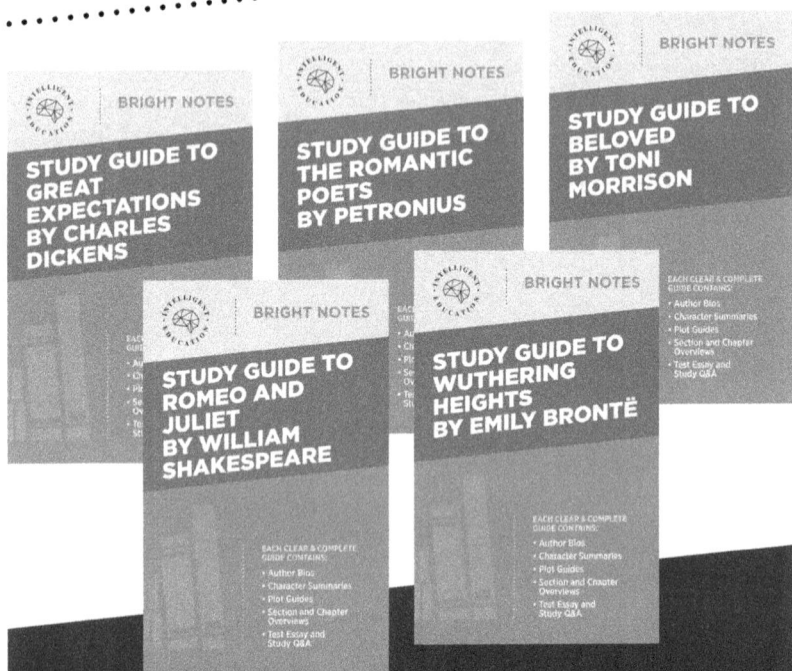

Lightning Source UK Ltd.
Milton Keynes UK
UKHW020638050922
408358UK00009B/1007